DIARY OF AN AIRBORNE RANGER

DIARY OF AN AIRBORNE RANGER

A LRRP's Year in the Combat Zone

Frank Johnson

BALLANTINE BOOKS • NEW YORK

INTRODUCTION

Diary of an Airborne Ranger is indeed a unique literary work. It is the day-by-day story of a nineteen-year-old youth's one-year odyssey into manhood. It is unique because it is not written in the perspective of an aging veteran recalling his warrior years through memories and recollections softened and mellowed by the ravages of time. Frank Johnson's diary is the compelling and refreshingly honest portrayal of a young man's introduction to war, with all the fearless bravado, unquestioned patriotism, intense loyalty, raw courage, and lost innocence that one can get only from being there. There are no pretenses here. What you see is exactly what you get.

When Frank Johnson arrived in South Vietnam in the fall of 1969, the war, for all intents and purposes, had already peaked. "Vietnamization" was the new buzz word, and Richard Nixon was keeping his promise by announcing troop withdrawals and a reduction in U.S. forces. To those of us who were there, the first indications of an army betrayed were just beginning to surface. No longer was there talk of defeating the enemy and achieving a just and final victory. Withdrawing with honor and grace became an acceptable alternative. To those young men just arriving in-country came the impossible task of covering our "withdrawal." They knew that they would never savor the laurels of total victory. There would be no parades, nor would they be welcomed home in the end. They knew all of this, yet they still volunteered to perform this impossible task.

Their actual mission was threefold: 1) to keep the enemy at bay by continuing to carry out offensive operations; 2) to provide for a smooth and orderly transition of U.S. weapons and equipment to our allies, along with the training and support to enable them to deploy it; and 3) to avoid alarming our allies by having them discover that they were in all actuality being abandoned.

Under these somewhat stressful conditions, Frank Johnson and his teammates were ordered to take the war to the enemy. Unlike their predecessors, the long-range reconnaissance patrollers whose primary mission was to gather intelligence, the Rangers were told to go out and initiate contact with the enemy. The army doctrine behind this gross misuse of five- to twelve-man reconnaissance teams was the doctrine of "force multipliers." Simply put, this meant to do more and risk less with smaller numbers of soldiers. The obvious benefit to our side was experiencing fewer friendly casualties while still maintaining an acceptable attrition rate among enemy personnel. The detriment was solely to the soldiers tasked to accept the risk. Remember, this was an increasingly unpopular war back home. Frank Johnson and his fellow Rangers were just such soldiers.

As you read through the pages of this amazing work you will find yourself wondering, "Why did they keep going back out and doing what they did?" The answer will surprise you. You see, it was not that same sense of duty and honor that had brought many of them into the service. It was not the same patriotism that had inspired their fathers and grandfathers before them. And it was definitely not power nor the promise of wealth that sent these young men into harm's way, day after day, even when they knew the war was already lost. "Why then," you ask? Well, let me tell you! It was camaraderie, the love that one teammate has for another. It was their motto, "Rangers don't leave Rangers behind!" This was not only their motto, but the guiding force that dictated their ethics, their courage, and their loyalty to one another. Can you understand the power of such feelings . . . the emotion? It is a powerful motivator.

Throughout Frank Johnson's diary, the recurring theme of camaraderie, brotherly love, and living up to the Ranger motto is demonstrated. This was a glorious thing that all warriors experienced to some degree or another during the Vietnam War, perhaps to a greater extent among the small, elite special-operations units that so often stood alone. When you read through each page of this book, forgive the language and the style—the author was just a kid out of high school when he penned it. There will be no literary awards or prizes coming his way. But if you want to understand what heroes are made of, and why so many of our young men come home with emotional baggage they can never shed, then read this book from cover to cover. When you're finished, go back and read it again—more slowly the second time. All of the emotions, the pain, and the memories, both good and bad, are right there. We know where they are. You'll have to find them for yourselves.

Gary A. Linderer
F Company, 58th Infantry (LRP)
L Company, 75th Infantry (Ranger)
101st Airborne Division
RVN 1968–1969

RANGERS LEAD THE WAY!

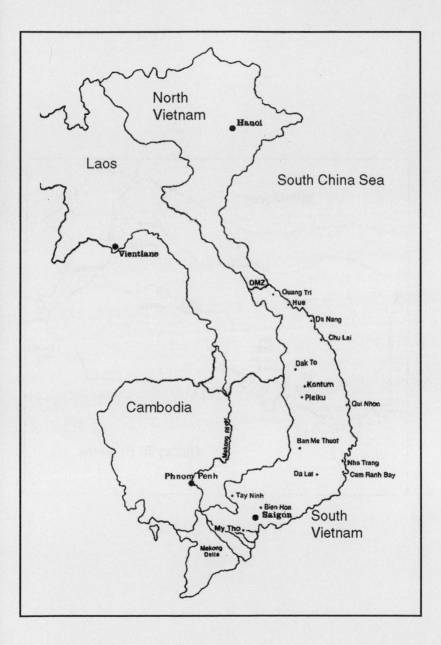

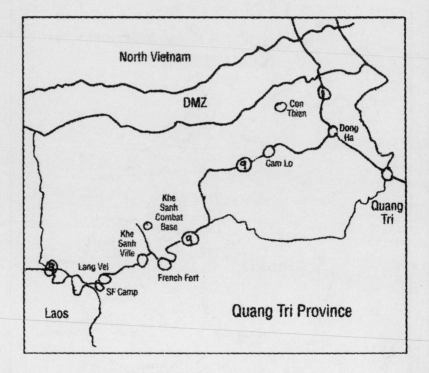

DIARY OF AN AIRBORNE RANGER

A LRRP's Year in the Combat Zone

I'm writing this diary because I don't want to write my family and tell them what I'm doing. I don't want them to worry. Today I met Gregg McGhee in San Francisco. We drove around for the last time in civilian land in an attempt to find what might be our last fling. But it was in vain. We spent the night at Gregg's grandparents'.

31 August 1969/Sunday

We arrived at Oakland Army Base at noon. I'm really excited. We drew all our combat gear, except weapons. We leave for Vietnam Tuesday.

02 September 1969/Tuesday

I called my parents and Pam before I left. It was really sad. It wasn't so bad with Pam, but it hurt to say good-bye to my parents. I expected my mom to cry, but it broke me up when Dad cried. I tried to assure them that I would be back and not to worry. I really don't think I'll die. And I will be back, as sure as my name is Frank Johnson!

04 September 1969/Thursday

Arrived in sweltering hot Bien Hoa, Vietnam at 1100. The heat just hits you right in the face. It's like California, but far more intense. Was great to see Vietnam from the air. It's really beautiful here. Everything is so green. The skies were fairly clear and we could see what looked like bombs exploding in the distance. I asked an officer who was on his second tour if somebody was being hit, and he said yes.

We were taken by bus to the 90th Replacement Battalion. It was a fun ride. The bus didn't have any glass in the windows but all of the windows were covered with wire to keep grenades from being thrown in on us. I wondered what was protecting the bottom of the bus. We passed several bombed-out buildings, and there were kids playing all over. The streets were very crowded with people and vehicles. It was like downtown Los Angeles during rush hour. But I wasn't expecting the simplicity and poverty of the place. I really like it here.

I was told today that I'm being assigned to the 101st Airborne Division, but Gregg is assigned to the 196th (Light Infantry Brigade, part of the Americal Division). I tried to get him to see about being transferred with me, but he wouldn't. He's really scared.

08 September 1969/Monday

We've got five days' refresher training called "P Training," before we all go to our assigned units. There were
some people recruiting for snipers and long-range reconnaissance patrols (LRRPs). The snipers work in two-man
teams and are attached to MACV. The LRRPs work in 5-
to 12-man teams called RTs (recon teams). Each Army
division has its own LRRP company. Sgt. Chambers
came from the LRRPs and was really impressive. I
wanted to go with the snipers, but I was more impressed
with Sgt. Chambers than the guy from the snipers. So I
volunteered for the LRRPs. Sgt. Chambers asked me if I
wanted to know what the life expectancy of a LRRP was
in combat. I said it didn't really matter, that war is unpre-
dictable, and that when my time is up, there is nothing I
can do about it. He said he liked my attitude, that I might
be okay.

I'm the only one who volunteered for an elite unit. All
the guys said I'm crazy. Even the captain I talked with on
the plane asked me if I knew what I was doing. He said I
was crazy. This is his second tour and he's going to be an
advisor. You know, I don't care what people say. I came
here to fight. I have been wanting to do this since I was a
kid. Now I'm going to do it with the LRRPs!

13 September 1969/Saturday

Training is over. It was pretty stupid. The only thing exciting that happened was we were hit with three 82mm mortar rounds Wednesday night. The hootch next to mine took a direct hit and had three killed. Everybody in my hootch hit the ground and began hiding. But I stayed in my rack. They all said now they know I'm crazy. I just lay there and listened. I told them that there is no place to hide or run to. No one here has a gun. If we take a hit, we're all dead. It would sure be a shame to die before ever getting to see the enemy. They all said I'm nuts.

14 September 1969/Sunday

I flew out of Bien Hoa on a Chinook helicopter and arrived at the LRRPs. The LRRPs have had their designation changed, now they're called Rangers. I'm stationed at Camp Eagle, which is six miles south of Hue and a little over 4½ miles north of Phu Bai. Which is all located in I Corps (the northernmost of Vietnam's four corps tactical zones). Hue is the capital of the northern part of South Vietnam, and is called the Imperial City.

I flew into Phu Bai and was driven to Camp Eagle. The base is huge, and contains all of the 101st Airborne Division, except one unit. The base is about 3½ miles long by almost 1½ miles wide, and about one mile off Highway 1. Highway 1 is the major road that runs the whole length of North and South Vietnam, along the coast. It's sort of like Highway 101 in California.

My unit is Co. L, 75th Infantry (Ranger). We are descendants of Merrill's Marauders, and are the eyes and ears of the 101st. We are attached to 2/17th CAV, because we use their slicks, gunships, and their Blues (quick-reaction infantry) for support when in contact. The Rangers are made up of an HQ platoon, a supply platoon, a communications platoon, and two field platoons. There are six teams per platoon. I'm in the Second Platoon. S.Sgt. Jefferson (a big Negro) is my platoon sergeant. We hit it off right away. He said that Sgt. Chambers spoke highly of me, that I've got potential, and for S.Sgt. Jefferson not to mess me up. The commanding officer of the company is Captain Guy, and the first sergeant is Bob Gilbert.

I was told by S.Sgt. Jefferson that now that I'm out of

that bullshit P Training, I will begin my real training classes here, to learn to work as a Ranger. S.Sgt. Jefferson said he'll see if I can measure up to Sgt. Chambers' expectations by the time the classes are over. He said he can't wait to see how a white kid from the streets of L.A. will act when the bullets start flying. I told him he might be impressed. He laughed and said I was a pretty cocky cherry (someone who hasn't been in combat).

17 September 1969/Wednesday

Sgt. Andy Ransom joined us from the Tiger Force. We hit it off right away. The Tigers have a pretty tuff reputation as an aggressive unit. We met another guy named Burgess C. Wetta. Everybody thought he and I were brothers when I first got here because we look alike. But "Burg" is an inch taller and 10 to 15 pounds heavier. He was little All-American as a quarterback in football and pitcher in baseball, in junior college.

19 September 1969/Friday

Burg's recon team was infilled by rappel and he got hurt when he fell on a downed tree. He has a bad back from a football injury, and reinjured it today.

What a fight! There is usually an initiation for cherries, but I went through mine tonight. Andy and I went to a show at the (Cavalry's) A Troop amphitheater. Two guys behind us kept making wisccracks about the Rangers, calling us names, etc. I got pissed and told them to shut up before they got hurt. They told me to go to hell. So I stood up and said, "Not before you!" This one guy (didn't know he was so big) told me to sit down, then pushed me. I fell onto the guy below me and he hit me in the chest. I hit him twice in the face with a left-right combination, and he fell. I then turned to the big guy and grabbed him by his shirt and jerked him down so that he fell to the bottom of the bleachers, four rows down. I then jumped on top of him and began hammering on his face. One of his friends jumped me, knocking me off. I hit that guy with a left, knocking him away. Another came at me and I left-kicked him in the stomach. Then another grabbed me from behind, pinning my arms to my side. Sgt. Davis, Polar Bear, and some other Rangers there came to my rescue. I jerked the guy holding me, throwing him to the ground, and Polar Bear hit and kicked him. Davis hit another guy on his head with his CAR-15 (a short-barreled M-16).

Sgt. Davis then told everybody to back off or they would have to deal with him and Polar Bear. Davis then asked if I thought I could take the big guy, because if I couldn't, then P. Bear would. I said we'll see. Davis said that if I'm losing, that P. Bear will take him out. The big guy and I then went at it. By the time this lieutenant broke it up, the guy's nose and mouth were bleeding. I'd only been hit a couple of times. The lieutenant began cussing us Rangers out, not even trying to listen to what happened. He threatened to call the MPs. Then he grabbed my shirt and I immediately snapped his elbow and hit him with a right in the face.

Davis grabbed me and we all beat feet to the company. It was really neat. The guys took me to our company club and bought me beer. They said after all this, I won't need an initiation.

20 September 1969/Saturday

That lieutenant and the big guy came to our company with two jeeps of MPs looking for me. I hid and Captain Guy said I'd gone to the field this AM. Captain Guy then grabbed me and I explained what happened. He then opened the bar and bought me a beer. He said I had broken the big guy's nose and knocked out a tooth, and broke the lieutenant's arm and gave him a fat lip.

Davis is a Negro who is a team leader (TL), and Polar Bear is a big white boy who is Davis' assistant team leader (ATL). I was told that a little while ago some of Davis' recon team members had gotten arrested by the MPs and put into jail here at Eagle. The commanding officer wouldn't or couldn't get them out, and Davis was scheduled to go to the field. So Davis took three of his recon team members and lined them outside the MP station, across the street, pointing his CAR-15 at the station. Davis then went inside and demanded his troops. The MPs told him to tamp sand, so Davis placed a frag on the counter, pulled the pin, and stated he wanted his troops or he was going to blow the building and take them. The MPs released the guys and they all beat feet back to the company and left for the field.

Apparently the commanding officer caught hell for that, but nothing came of it. Now the zips come to our area of operations in force, when they have to, and only when they have to. Our company area of operations is fenced off from the rest of the compound, with barbed-wire fence. And nobody enters without going through the company headquarters and without the commanding officer's permission, because we are a top-secret unit.

21 September 1969/Sunday

I've been bugging S.Sgt. Jefferson about going to the field. So he finally got sick of me asking. I'm going out with Passmore's recon team tomorrow. S.Sgt. Jefferson said the commanding officer told him to send me out so he won't be bugged by that lieutenant I'd fought with. The commanding officer said I've got to get all this energy out of me before I end up in a cage. All this last week I've been put on labor duty, going outside the perimeter and filling sandbags, and going through classes. On one run for sandbags, a bunch of us going to a dirt pile were met by a bunch of kids and some teenage girls. A mamasan (older Vietnamese woman) asked if any of us wanted to have sex with her daughter, because "she wants to have a big baby boy." I guess a couple guys went, but I didn't. The girl looked really young.

The classes I went through were pretty neat. One lesson that really stood out, and that the guys pushed, was our motto, "Rangers don't leave Rangers behind!" Passmore took us cherries out into the street and worked on IADs, immediate-action drills. That meant how to react to common danger situations in the bush, "contact right," "contact left," "contact front," etc. and some dos and don'ts. The training was pretty neat, and I'm really excited about going out.

22 September 1969/Monday

1st Mission–Portugal–YD5222

We're radio relay, parked on an old firebase called Helen.
The recon team is made up of:

Team Leader: Passmore
Assistant Team Leader: Glasser
Radio/Telephone Operator (RTO): Me
Assistant RTO: Morrow ("Jew")
Scout: Rodarte
Slack: Andy Ransom

23 September 1969/Tuesday

Jew spotted a VC on the top of the hill we were on. I don't think we were spotted. There is supposed to be a sapper company (enemy engineers, who specialize in demolitions and base infiltration) at the base of the hill we're on.

25 September 1969/Thursday

We were told to stay for one more day, so a light observation helicopter (LOH, pronounced "loach") came to resupply us. But its rotors hit a tree and it crashed. One guy was hurt but they were all lucky they weren't KIA (killed in action). I took a picture of the guy WIA (wounded in action) and he made it look dramatic. The Blues—the Cav's quick-reaction "air rifle" infantry platoon—came in and covered while some engineers blew up the LOH, because they couldn't lift it out (and didn't want to leave it as salvage for the enemy). Despite all the ruckus we had made, we were left in the field. Lieutenant Johnson, the 1st Platoon leader, stayed with us.

26 September 1969/Friday

Exfilled. I've been assigned to Sgt. Karalow's recon team, along with Andy. Karalow is pretty cool, but his tour is almost up. Our recon team is recon team 24, the Bushwhackers:

TL: Karalow
ATL: Sgt. Ed Drozd
RTO: Me
Assistant RTO: Sp4. John Strope
Point: Sgt. Andy Ransom
Weapons: PFC Michael Lytle

29 September 1969/Monday

2d Mission—Arabia

I've been lagging behind on this diary. I'm pretty lazy when it comes to writing. I have to get into the writing mode.

30 September 1969/Tuesday

It started raining at 1800 yesterday and hasn't let up since. It's raining really hard, and hard to keep warm. John (Strope) isn't with us, so Scotty has taken his place. I thought the tropics were supposed to be warm all of the time.

02 October 1969/Thursday

End of four days of hell. It rained 43 inches since Monday. All the recon teams in the bush, including ours, got some kind of immersion foot. Scotty got it real bad and had to go to the hospital. He'll be down for quite a while. Passmore told me to always carry at least one extra pair of socks. I did and it saved me. My feet weren't too bad. I kept changing my socks, wringing them out and putting the wet pair inside my shirt to dry them and help stay warm. It was cold when I first put them in my shirt, but actually it kept me pretty warm.

06 October 1969/Monday

3d Mission–Korea–ZD1508

We had three days of rest then we were back at it. Our area of operations is at the beach. We're going to try to find a company of VC who are stealing rice from the villagers located south of us.

This last week (04 October 1969/Saturday) we had four Aussie LRRPs (SAS) at our company looking to do some recruiting. They were pretty neat. They work in four-man recon teams and carry sten guns. They were all over six feet tall. Jordan said he had a lot of respect for them, but he is about to DEROS (rotate back to the States) and plans on joining the Israeli army when he gets back to the World. Jordan is a pretty neat guy. He's shorter than me, but heavier, with wide shoulders. He says he likes it here, but wants to join the Israelis.

07 October 1969/Tuesday

It rained all last night and forced us to sleep sitting on our rucks (backpacks). Just before light, I felt something crawling on my right thumb. I smashed it and the bugger stung the hell out of me! I almost screamed, it hurt so bad. It felt like my thumb was as big as a softball. I was finally able to shrug it off and went back to sleep. A few minutes later, I felt it crawling on my neck, trying to get into my shirt. I was afraid to smash it with it right next to my neck, so I let it crawl down onto my right chest. I thought if I hit it as hard as I can, I can KIA it. So I went for the big smash and the bitch stung me twice on my chest! I'd knocked the wind right out of myself! By now it was getting light, and I see this little brown scorpion run out of my shirt, onto my leg, and jump into the bush! My chest felt as big as a basketball. Neither my hand or my chest actually swelled up, but it sure felt like it.

Then, to top it off, an ant colony decided to make a new home in my ruck! I spent twenty minutes cleaning them out. I told the recon team about the scorpion so we'll see if I get sick or die. That would be a pisser to be killed in Vietnam by an NVA scorpion! "Frank Johnson, KIA during an engagement with one NVA scorpion." A great epitaph!!!

09 October 1969/Thursday

End of mission and I survived the NVA scorpion. It must have been a VC scorpion. Sure was a beautiful area of operations, but no bad guys.

13 October 1969/Monday

4th Mission

I forgot again. It's pretty bad when I'm the RTO. I just keep forgetting to write this down. I didn't put this entry in until the 18th.

16 October 1969/Thursday

End of mission. Nothing happened, just a lot of humping. Lytle left our recon team and is with Sgt. Dave Bennett's recon team. S.Sgt. Bates arrived today. He's an old buddy from NCO and Ranger school. It's great to see him. I've always liked him a lot.

18 October 1969/Saturday

I've got this thing with the Lord that if I lose my cross, it's a sign from Him that I'm going to die. I'm not religious, but I know God is real and I asked Him to use my cross as a sign. I lost it while watching a movie tonight at the A-Troop amphitheater. I was with Sp4. Robin Kristiansen and Andy Ransom. I'm always touching it, so I discovered it was missing during the show. When the lights came on, I told Robin and Andy that I lost it and we began looking for it. I told them about my prayer, so we retraced our steps back to the company, but couldn't find it.

Well, if God wants me, I guess I'm going. I just pray I'm not a baby when I go. Sure is a shame to get into only one firefight and then die without being able to experience anything. But when God wants you, He wants you. At least I know and will try and make this a good one and not let my recon team down.

19 October 1969/Sunday

5th Mission—Norway—Tennessee Valley

What a fitting day to die, on a Sunday! Last night, I told Dennis about my cross so he said we would be extra careful. We infilled at 1000 and found a high-speed trail (wide, flat, suitable for easy movement) right off the landing zone. We followed it up the hill for two hundred to three hundred yards, until noon. We stopped for lunch and set up five yards off the trail, with Drozd sitting next to a tree on the trail. Dennis had told everybody about my cross, so everybody was being extra careful.

Twenty minutes later we heard NVA talking and laughing. Dennis and I looked up and spotted three NVA just twenty yards away, eating chow! We had been so careful that we walked within twenty yards of them and they didn't even know it! Dennis asked me what I thought we should do. I said let's go for a POW. He said okay and said get on the radio and tell headquarters so they know what we're about to do and will be here when we need them. I got on the radio and had to talk very quietly so the NVA wouldn't hear me. It was really hard for headquarters to hear me. But I finally got it across to HQ with the help of another recon team. All of a sudden, the NVA got up and began to move in our direction. The point man moved out five yards ahead of the other two. Dennis and I didn't see them move, when all of a sudden shots were fired from Drozd's position. We couldn't see Drozd because of the thickness of the bush, and thought that either he was shot or had opened up on the NVA on his own.

Dennis and I both started to get up and run to Drozd when the other two NVA opened up on us. The rounds went right under my chin, kicking dirt into my face and forcing me back. Dennis and I then threw frags, WIA the two NVA. Dennis then opened up with his CAR-15 on auto while I got on the radio and called in the contact. I told them we only had the three in sight, and didn't know what was above them, thinking that there might be more NVA with them.

The other two NVA beat feet then and we went to Drozd. Drozd had heard the NVA and when the one NVA walked up to him, he put three rounds into the NVA's head. The rest of the recon team didn't know what was going on because of the thickness of the bush. Dennis and I didn't want to make any more noise until we figured out what we were going to do. We got two 50-pound bags of rice containing payroll for the unit the NVA were going to, and some orders. We also got one AK-47 from the KIA. Losing the cross was a warning from God! Thanks, God, for watching out for me and my guys!

A fast mover (a jet) arrived and dropped two napalm on the top of the hill, just in case there were more NVA. Then the Blues arrived with a dog-tracker team. We found two blood trails, but no more NVA. It was really hot out, and the dogs just about died on us. I'd caught a small piece of shrapnel in my left shoulder, but didn't know it until one of the Blues saw the bloodstream running down my arm. I pulled out the sliver, then we walked back to our landing zone and exfilled.

When we were walking by this tree in the middle of where the napalm had been dropped, I found a three-foot-long light-green iguana on the tree. A Kit Carson Scout (former Viet Cong soldiers who volunteered to work with

American units) with the Blues said the iguana is good eating but we let it live since it had survived the napalm. Dennis came up to me later and said I had a great rapport with God. One of the guys said I have "vision."

20 October 1969/Monday

6th Mission–SAME

We were sent back to the same area of operations but without Andy. He went to Recondo School (a "finishing school" for LRRPs run by the 5th Special Forces in Nha Trang). S.Sgt. Salters is taking Andy's place. We infilled with the Blues and then they left after a short while, and we stayed. It's called a stay-behind mission. We set an ambush on the trail for the night.

Walder's recon team met an NVA on a trail but the NVA got away with no fire exchanged.

23 October 1969/Thursday

End of mission. Was pretty dull. We were hoping to find the NVA that had gotten away, but no luck.

26 October 1969/Sunday

7th Mission–Mali

I've been loafing on this diary again. Some of it I don't write until days later. This project will be a dud if I don't keep it up. It's really okay right now because nothing's going on.

29 October 1969/Wednesday

End of mission. It's odd without Andy being with us; you get attached to some people. It's like we knew each other and we just click. I miss him.

Bennett's recon team was in contact. They E-and-E'd (escaped and evaded) down a hill and had to cross a river. While crossing, Lytle was swept downriver and KIA, and they lost all their equipment. Apparently Lytle panicked in the swift current because he couldn't swim. He lost his footing and was swept away. He was found later quite a ways downriver.

31 October 1969/Friday

8th Mission–Yugoslavia

I swear this will be the last time I forget!!!

03 November 1969/Monday

End of mission.

S.Sgt. Black in contact. They KIA one NVA and found a cache of 22 122mm rockets.

04 November 1969/Tuesday

Black stayed in yesterday and made contact again today, KIA one more NVA. Black has the reputation of being one of the best team leaders in the company. Black is about six foot or six-one, and stocky. I was told a story that on one mission Black set an ambush on a trail. He wanted a POW, so he waited off the trail while his recon team set up to cover him. Two NVA came diddy-boppin' down the trail and Black jumped on one while the other ran away. When Black jumped on the NVA's back, the NVA flipped Black onto the ground, hit him, then beat feet. Black's recon team was so stunned that they didn't even fire a shot!

Black and I don't seem to get along, so I didn't ask him if it was true. I still think he is a pretty good team leader though. I would like to go out with him to learn. But Black is in the 1st Platoon and I'm in the 2d. The platoon recon teams aren't mixed that I know of. When the recon teams are combined, it's usually within the platoons.

06 November 1969/Thursday

9th Mission–Sleeping Beauty–YC7982

We're heavy (i.e., two teams combined) with S.Sgt. Solko's recon team. Solko was my instructor when I went through Ranger training.

07 November 1969/Friday

Drozd, Strope, and I went on a recon this AM. We were just coming to a clearing when a landing-zone watcher (a Viet Cong or NVA soldier detailed to watch a probable landing zone that could be used by American troops) opened up on us from our right, firing three rounds. The first round grazed the bottom of my chin and hit the first-aid pouch on my left shoulder, completely destroying it. The second round went between Drozd and Strope, and the third went behind Strope. Drozd immediately pulled me down, then we all opened up, but the NVA beat feet. It happened so suddenly that I didn't realize we'd made contact even though the round grazed my chin, until Drozd pulled me down. I was too busy moving with the concussion of the round against my face. It left a scab on my chin, but didn't bleed.

08 November 1969/Saturday

We went to where the landing zone watcher had opened up on us. The NVA had been sitting in a clump of bushes, next to a high-speed trail, right off a probable landing zone. The trail was heading right up the hill so we followed it for a little ways. But it was too socked in for us to go very far. It's for sure we would have made contact, but the clouds were too low for help to come and bail us out. It has been raining since we got out here.

The NVA left his tracks on the trail. We went back to where the NVA was sitting and will see what comes of it. We'll let the NVA come to us. We're in the Ruong Ruong Valley. This is where the NVA come to meet for their offensives. The Ruong Ruong is as bad as the Tennessee Valley. Beaucoup NVA, just about any time you want them.

10 November 1969/Monday

End of mission. It rained too hard to do any good. The slick had a hard time getting us out, with all of the rain and low clouds. If it hadn't been raining, there was a pretty good chance we would have made contact.

13 November 1969/Thursday

10th Mission—Ajax—YC8288

We're heavy, with S.Sgt. Davis' recon team. Polar Bear has DEROS'd and Karalow is on extension leave (leave granted when a soldier extended his tour of duty in Vietnam), so Drozd is our team leader and Sgt. Tom Horne is our assistant team leader. Horne and I have become pretty good friends, but he's the kind that if you piss him off at the wrong time, it doesn't make any difference who you are to him. He'll come after you. He stands about six-two or six-three, and is pretty strong. He and I are alternating at point. He has today.

14 November 1969/Friday

We found an old NVA camp on Hill 356. We went north and found a fresh rest area with eight sleeping positions. There were punji stakes surrounding the camp. It's sitting right on a three-way trail junction. We've got a Kit Carson Scout, named Ut, with us who says we're in the middle of an NVA base camp area. Sgt. Horne and I wanted to set an ambush here, but this is Davis' last mission, and he wants to get home in one piece. Anyway, Ut is brand new to us and Davis doesn't trust him. But I kind of like the guy. Apparently he's an ex–seven-year NVA.

We went back to Hill 356, with me at point, and I found a .51-cal. booby trap that we had missed earlier and somehow didn't set off. I kept the round.

15 November 1969/Saturday

This AM we found two hootches. They were both 20 feet
by 40 feet and both had a bunker under the hard-packed
dirt floor. Davis is really nervous. He thinks we might not
make it out of this area of operations because of all the
signs of NVA everywhere we turn. Even Ut is nervous,
saying there is beaucoup NVA here. I told Davis I would
take care of him and make sure he gets out of here in one
piece. But he doesn't want any part of this mission. It's
just "short timer's nerves." Davis is really a good dude.

16 November 1969/Sunday

We found another hootch that is bigger than the other two. This one has three rooms with a bunker under the kitchen. The signs of NVA are really fresh. Ut is just shrugging his shoulders.

17 November 1969/Monday

End of mission. A lot of fresh signs all over the place, but not one NVA. Would be a great area to go back into for a POW or just an ambush.

Lt. (David) Ohle arrived today as our new 2d Platoon leader.

21 November 1969/Friday

11th Mission–Nutmeg–YC5193

We're heavy, with Solko's recon team again, but Solko isn't with us because he developed sores, so he's grounded. We also have a new cherry named S.Sgt. McElroy. He's really a sorry dude. He just completed Ranger School, but doesn't know his butt from a hole in the ground. Maybe it's just because he's new, but I doubt it. Mac is assigned to my recon team. For this mission we have two Special Forces (SF) guys with us, one a medic and the other a commo guy. They have joined CCN (Command and Control North, part of the Studies and Observation Group—SOG—supersecret cross-border recon program) and they're with us for training. They're pretty cool guys. The medic is really funny. I hope they do okay during their tour. I like them. When they finish with us, they'll be assigned to a CCN recon team.

22 November 1969/Saturday

We found a well-used trail with wooden steps going up this really steep hill. If it wasn't for the miserable rain, we might find some NVA.

Suzi Delanoy's birthday (twenty-one) [first cousin].

25 November 1969/Tuesday

End of mission. We had a real freak show on the landing zone. Lieutenant Johnson said he was on his way to exfill us, so we blew down two trees with claymores and fired a LAW. Johnson didn't show until four hours later! Good thing the NVA were hiding from the rain. Was neat to see what a claymore does to a tree though.

27 November 1969/Thursday

We had a big company Thanksgiving party. It was the first time the whole company has been together. I met guys I haven't seen before. Some of these guys are crazy! I think I'm going to like it here. I got wasted on rum and coke. Dave Weeks had to help me to my hootch.

04 December 1969/Thursday

I left for MACV Recondo School today with a bunch of guys. We made it to Cam Ranh Bay. We are going to get rooms at a hotel in Nha Trang this weekend and get us some girls!

05 December 1969/Friday

We arrived in Nha Trang and we all got rooms at the Nha Trang Hotel. We then went around to some whorehouses and each got a girl for the night. Mine's name is Cam, from Cambodia. She's a real chump. I'll get rid of her tomorrow.

06 December 1969/Saturday

I got rid of Cam and went around to five different houses until I finally picked My, also from Cambodia. She's really pretty and very polite. She treats me like I'm the only one in the world. Al and his girl and My and I toured Nha Trang together. We went to the beaches and all over the town. We had a great time. We then went to a movie and Al and I were the only round-eyes in the theater. I thought we might get into a fight, but it didn't develop. The movies were in Vietnamese with English subtitles. It was fun. My wants me to come back and see her when I get out of school.

07 December 1969/Sunday

We reported to school today. It's run by SF, and all of the instructors are former Command and Control recon team members. Nha Trang is SF headquarters.

We were divided into recon teams and I'm assistant team leader of my recon team. My instructor is SFC (sergeant first class, paygrade E-7) Thompson. One of the guys on my recon team is this black guy, Sp4. John Sherman, a Ranger from N Company, 75th Infantry (Ranger), attached to the 173d Airborne. We became very good friends. He's our point man. Only Rangers, Special Forces, SEALs, and Marine Corps Force Recon and like that go to this school.

09 December 1969/Tuesday

From 0500 to 0600 is PT. We run with 30-pound rucks, rifle, and web gear. We run a mile, increasing a mile each day until we're running seven miles. But because of Christmas, we'll only have to run four miles. I carry 32 magazines on my web gear, where most carry about 21 magazines. The extra weight is heavy! We can't change our combat loads, so I'm stuck with what I have. We should have had classes at my company before I showed up here. I would have left some of my gear at the company.

12 December 1969/Friday

I don't think I'm going to finish this school. I'm fifth in
the run and in the top 5 percent in PT, but my classroom
work sucks. I can't seem to get into the class work. I was
never good in school anyway, and even though I'm really
into what is being taught, I am having a hard time buck-
ling down. I have a hard time paying attention. The instructor will hit on something that deals with the bush
and I begin to daydream about missions. There are tests
throughout, and I've gotten below a 70% on two tests.
You are only allowed to flunk three tests and you're history. There are two phase exams, with Phase One coming
up on the 14th. I have to pass the Phase One.

15 December 1969/Monday

Well, I passed the Phase One with an 86%, but I only have a 69% average. You have to have at least a 70% to stay. They were going to kick me out, but I've been put on trial. But only because physically I've been impressive. I've moved to third physically and I was told that the 101st Rangers have a great reputation with the school. Anyway, it's Christmas and I have potential. It's also my birthday on graduation day.

17 December 1969/Wednesday

Luchow's recon team in contact. No KIA.

I'm really having a ball here. There is a recon team of Korean LRRPs, and about every night they work out with Hwa Rang Do karate. I was watching them and they asked me if I wanted to train with them. For the last five days I've been getting my butt kicked by them. I'm having a lot of fun though. These guys really seem to like me. The team leader of the Koreans is their fastest in the runs, and I've been running with him up until about the last mile or so, then he leaves me behind. He's second fastest in the school, I'm third, and I can't seem to keep up with him. I guess they really like me because I acknowledge them and show an interest.

19 December 1969/Friday

Solko's recon team had gotten socked in and couldn't get out. They spent a record ten days in the bush.

Luchow's recon team in contact again, and again no KIA.

23 December 1969/Tuesday

Graduated from Recondo School. It was a lot of fun, but real hard for me. I struggled through the class work, but ended with an 85%. Sherman really helped me with the class work. I excelled in the PT and in the bush exercise. We went on a three-day mission on Hon Tre Island, but it was a dud. There was supposed to be a sapper unit on the island, but I think they just told us that to keep our interest.

Sherman and I had to get up in front of the whole class and sing "Green Green Grass of Home" because we knocked country and western music, which the Special Forces soldiers swear by. It was really fun because we stylized it by acting like the Temptations. The instructors booed us and kicked us off the stage, but everybody else thought it was really funny.

A lieutenant from the First CAV Rangers got best student and won the Gerber commando knife (given as a prize to the best student). John and I didn't think he was so great. He didn't show us anything tactics-wise. All he was was gung ho. I went to the SF HQ and asked about joining CCN (Command and Control North). They said they have changed commanding officers and are running their recon teams with four or five indigenous and one American. They are pulling the same kind of missions we are, but they get to cross the border into Laos and they work with Yards (indigenous mountain peoples) and Nungs (Chinese). I decided to stay with the Rangers. I feel that if I go now, I'd be letting the Rangers down. "Rangers don't leave Rangers behind"!

The guys went to Saigon for a few days, but I caught a flight to Phu Bai and then rode into Eagle. I didn't want to go to Saigon because I felt like I was going to miss out on something. Pretty stupid! But I just want to go out to the bush. My recon team goes out tomorrow as a matter of fact. Good timing.

My birthday (20).

24 December 1969/Wednesday

12th Mission–Mercury–YD3602

Heavy, with Horne's recon team.
  Jeff's birthday (14) [brother].

25 December 1969/Thursday

MERRY CHRISTMAS!!! May God be with us and protect us the rest of our tour!

26 December 1969/Friday

Rodarte's recon team made contact two klicks from us. No KIA.

Bob Hope came to Eagle today, but I'm here on this dud of a mission, missing the show. If I'd have gone to Saigon with the guys after Recondo School, I would have been able to see Bob Hope. Bob Hope is one of the attractions I wanted to see while I was in Vietnam. But I missed it over this dud mission!

27 December 1969/Saturday

End of mission. We found three NVA campsites, one US fragmentation grenade, and two US helmets. There were a lot of signs, but no NVA.

28 December 1969/Sunday

Ski's recon team was in heavy contact. Three of his recon team are wounded, one seriously, and will be going home. No NVA KIA!

29 December 1969/Monday

Dunkle's recon team (Fairlane) in contact. They got quite a few NVA KIA!

I got paid $281.00, of which $100.00 went into savings. Is this all I make for getting my butt shot at?

01 January 1970/Thursday

Chapman's recon team in contact. They got four WIA but killed three NVA. They are a klick from where I'm going tomorrow. I think Chapman freaked during his contact.

02 January 1970/Friday

13th Mission–Excalibur–YD0531

We're heavy, with Sgt. Dave Bennett's recon team. Bennett is from Huntington Beach, Ca. He's supposed to be one of the best on the radio. In one big contact his recon team had gotten into, Dave was running and ran right into a tree and knocked himself out. He got a Purple Heart!

06 January 1970/Tuesday

We were supposed to get out today, but it's raining too hard and the clouds are too low for the slicks to get to us.

08 January 1970/Thursday

End of a miserable seven days. It rained most of the time. But we did have a lot of fruit in the area of operations. Was a lot of banana trees and a fresh running creek. Was a beautiful area of operations. This was Drozd's and Bennett's last mission. They leave country in less than thirty days. I'll miss Drozd. He's a pretty funny dude, and was pretty good to us. I learned some things from him.

Dave Weeks' recon team made contact twice today. First they didn't get any KIA, but on their second contact they got one KIA. Everybody around us made contact but us!

11 January 1970/Sunday

A very sad day for us. S.Sgt. Salters' recon team made
contact today. It was raining real hard and was pretty
cold. So they were heating up some cocoa when the NVA
snuck up on them and opened up, KIA Salters, the team
leader, and Jones, the assistant team leader. It was pretty
hairy for a while because the recon team was unable to
exfil because of the low clouds and rain. A LOH finally
was able to get the recon team out, but could only take
two guys out at a time. When it got down to the last three
guys, Sgt. Brown was forced to stay behind by himself.
He was put in for the Distinguished Service Cross, along
with the LOH pilot, who did a fantastic job.

The whole recon team freaked and only the coolness
of the LOH pilot saved them. When Brown was left by
himself, he had attempted to grab the skids of the LOH.
But the LOH wouldn't get up because of the weight of
the three extra guys. So the gunner had to kick Brown off
the skids. So Brown didn't volunteer to stay behind, he
was kicked off the LOH and forced to stay. That doesn't
deserve a medal. What he did was not an act of bravery.
They were all lucky to be alive.

That was Jones' first and last mission. Salters had
been around for quite a while, and his death hit a lot of
the "Old Foul Dudes" pretty hard. I knew Salters only
briefly, and I really liked him. Isn't there a poem about
men and mice?

13 January 1970/Tuesday

Bates' and Stauffer's heavy recon team in contact. Yesterday they discovered they were sitting right next to an NVA base camp. Bates was grazed in the head and Blinston was hit in the hand. The wounds aren't serious. Beaucoup NVA KIA by the gunships. The grunts are going into the area of operations tomorrow.

14 January 1970/Wednesday

14th Mission–Malibu–XD9337

We have a new recon team now that Drozd is gone.
Recon team #24, Phantom Rangers:

    TL: Sgt. Andy Ransom
    ATL: me
    Radio: Sp4. Burgess Wetta
    PM: Sgt. Bruce Bowland
    PM: S.Sgt. McElroy

    Burg is finally with Andy and me. We are the "Insepa-
rable Three"!

17 January 1970/Saturday

Bates and Dunkle, heavy, had movement during the night, but nothing happened.

18 January 1970/Sunday

End of mission.
  (Kerry) Lee's birthday (21) [married older sister].

20 January 1970/Tuesday

McCoy and Horne, heavy, have spotted a convoy of elephants at the Laotian border, going into Vietnam.

21 January 1970/Wednesday
15th Mission–Dotson–XD8739

We're heavy, with Rodarte, monitoring the crossroads south of the old Marine base at Khe Sanh. We have two new cherries, S.Sgt. Norton, for Rodarte's recon team, and Sp4. Sorenson for us. Sorenson is really a sorry dude, and he has to be on my recon team!

23 January 1970/Friday

The combat base on Hill 1015 fired off several flares. Hill 1015 is a staging base for CCN recon teams. We then spotted sixteen air bursts to the west, at the Laotian border. It looked like either signals or checking range.

24 January 1970/Saturday

End of mission.

Bugsy Moran's and Rose's recon team, heavy, in contact. Rose, Kennedy, and Shortround were on a recon checking their back trail because they thought they were being followed. They spotted NVA trailing them, so they ambushed them, with Rose spraying one across the chest.

S.Sgt. Paige and S.Sgt. Bates, heavy, were being infilled by separate slicks, into the Ruong Ruong Valley. But the slicks got separated somehow. Bates was being infilled on top of a hill, overlooking the valley, while Paige was infilled onto the valley floor. So headquarters was going to leave them as they were, instead of picking up one recon team and placing it with the other. The damage was already done. They were supposed to recon the valley because there is supposed to be a meeting there of a large NVA force. But both recon teams are in contact. Both are taking heavy .51-cal. (heavy machine gun) and AK (automatic rifle) fire.

Paige is completely surrounded. A slick went in to get Bates, thirty minutes after his infil, barely getting him out. They KIA several NVA right on the landing zone, with the tail rotor buzzing off the head of one NVA! But no one could get to Paige because of the heavy fire. Paige then somehow broke free of the encirclement and beat feet, with the NVA hot on their heels. Twice Banshee 54 (call sign of Huey aircraft that rescued Paige's team in Ruong Ruong) attempted to exfil them, but failed each time because of the heavy fire and because it was getting dark. Paige infilled at 1700, and stayed in until 2400, when despite Colonel Molinelli's orders to abandon the recon team, Banshee 54 tried three more times to exfil the recon team, finally succeeding on the fourth try! The recon team was pulled under very heavy fire, barely making it out. The gunbirds KIA beaucoup NVA and only three Rangers were slightly WIA. A lot of the guys had rounds go right through their clothing, hitting their rucks, and kicking dirt and crap all around them. Too close! We almost lost both recon teams. Thanks, Lord, for being with them and bringing them out Okay!!! That pissant Molinelli was going to leave the recon team by themselves. He told them to dig in and make a perimeter and he would have flare ships flying over them, and then bring in a reaction force in the AM. What a piece of crap! The recon team would have been wiped out by morning! Maybe he should go out there and we'll wait until the AM to get him.

28 January 1970/Wednesday

16th Mission–Grizzly Bear–YC8584

We went in just west of the Ruong Ruong, close to where
Paige and Bates were. We went in on a ridge, then up the
ridge to another ridge, where we found a high-speed trail
with signs of use. The trail runs up and down the finger
we're on. We wanted to monitor the trail but stayed out of
sight, so I put us into some real thick bushes for our NDP
(night defensive perimeter).

At 2100, when it was my turn for watch, I spotted two
NVA with flashlights, trying to find our claymores. The
flashlights were really dull. They covered our whole
perimeter, but couldn't find our claymores. I very quietly
woke everybody up, and we just watched them. They finally tried to get us to give ourselves away by throwing
dirt clods. One hit me right in the forehead! I thought that
was really funny, and it was all I could do to keep from
laughing out loud. The NVA finally gave up and left. I
think that if there were more than just the two of them,
we would have been in a firefight. I wanted to go for a
POW, but these guys didn't want to because we didn't
know how many were actually out there, and we were a
ways away from the landing zone, and it was dark. I
really think we could have gotten them and got away with
it. Oh well, there will be other times. Anyway, we still
have tomorrow.

29 January 1970/Thursday

We called in a Pink Team (a Cavalry air-recon team consisting of a reconnaissance LOH, code-named "white" and a gunship escort code-named "red"—hence "pink" team) to look over the area of operations for us, but instead of looking, they shot the area of operations up. I yelled at them on the radio and they left. Nothing like letting the NVA know where you are! They probably think we're scared out of our drawers.

All day long we were being followed. We finally backtracked, then set up twenty-five yards off the trail and into some thick bush. We lost our shadows. I wanted to set an ambush on the trail, but no one else wanted to. They felt if we did, the NVA would be between us and our only landing zone out. But we can always run down the hill.

30 January 1970/Friday

No sign of the NVA. I guess we outfoxed them for now. We've got a real good NDP, so we'll stay here awhile and see what happens. You know, I'm really proud of how I outfoxed the NVA. I really did do a good job. I have found something I really like and am good at. At least so far. Now I'd like to see how I'd react to a really big or heavy firefight. The way this mission is going, I just might get my chance.

01 February 1970/Sunday

End of mission. We had to backtrack to the landing zone we infilled on, because it was the only landing zone in the area of operations. I continued to walk point until we got to the top of the hill, then took rear security because we were being followed again. We got out without any problems though. I guess we weren't much of a threat by hiding like we did.

Craig's birthday (13) [brother].

02 February 1970/Monday

Brad's birthday (18) [brother]. I'm sending him $25.00 and Craig my AM/FM radio.

05 February 1970/Thursday

17th Mission–Panther–YC8382

We have another cherry, PFC Parrot (18). He looks like he's only 16.

Two Marine Force Recon teams in contact in the A Shau Valley today. I recognized the radio operator as being in MACV Recondo school with me. He is also from Pomona, Ca. He stated they have four to six hundred "Little People" coming his way and asked what they should do. He was told to monitor them, and if they see him, to shoot them. By late afternoon, both recon teams were wiped out! Stinking stupid Marines. Why did they do that? The recon teams should have stayed hidden or beat feet and called all kinds of hell on the pissants. And piss on those guys in the rear who are sitting in their comfortable chairs armchair-quarterbacking! They don't have a clue what's going on and their asses aren't hanging out in the wind! Two whole recon teams gone! It was really sad to listen to. I kept yelling into the radio for them to get out of there, but it didn't do any good. It was bad!

06 February 1970/Friday

Horne's recon team in contact. They KIA two NVA and were pulled.

They were our radio relay. Now we don't have commo.

07 February 1970/Saturday

Damn Parrot brought a dead battery and Sorenson's extra battery is dead. Now we only have commo when Lieutenant Ohle is flying above us. It's my fault for not checking!

09 February 1970/Monday

End of mission. The slick landed on the landing zone before we got there and we had to sprint about 150 yards.

10 February 1970/Tuesday

Firebase Rifle was hit by 120 rockets and then overrun by a ground force. The NVA KIA six and WIA ten Americans, then just beat feet. Pretty weird. They had control of the whole base. I guess they didn't want to stick around and get strafed.

12 February 1970/Thursday

Bates' recon team in contact. Fowler was exfilled because of an injury to his knee, and that gave the recon team away. They KIA one NVA.

Mom's birthday (42).

13 February 1970/Friday

Hue took rocket fire last night. So far there have been three firebases and Hue hit by rockets and/or ground attack, and Eagle is right in the middle of it all.

16 February 1970/Monday

Yeck went out two days ago and found a hootch with four NVA. Since he is in a base camp area of operations, the Blues were going to go in and sweep the area. But Yeck has made contact and KIA five NVA. the Blues went in and swept the area of operations. Yeck stayed in and set an ambush.

17 February 1970/Tuesday

Bates' and my recon teams went to Quang Tri today because we're going out tomorrow. Bates and I went to P Company, Rangers, 5th Infantry Divison (Mechanized) and met with S.Sgts. Gates and Karres, who we both went through NCO and Ranger schools with. They said they are having a great time. They were looking good. Was good to see them. I pray they make it home okay.

18 February 1970/Wednesday

18th Mission—Puma—XD8945

When we're being infilled, I'm usually first off the slick and I like to jump from the slick before it hits the ground because I have a fear of getting hit and the slick crashing. It would hurt to crash in a slick and we're sitting ducks during infil and exfil. So I jumped when the slick was about ten feet off the ground and everybody followed. On the first day, our gear averages about a hundred pounds, so we can make quite a splash when we land. Well, Parrot did, and he broke his ankle and had to be exfilled. He left his rifle behind, so I broke it down and packed it in my ruck.

Andy and I went on a recon and found an old grunt firebase. It was a mess with trash and trashed gear all over the place. Looks like a dump site.

Yeck spotted two NVA today, but let them go.

19 February 1970/Thursday

We moved west and found the main firebase today. It had twenty-five bunkers with barbed wire all around it. It was still in fairly good shape, except that the weeds needed to be cleaned away.

20 February 1970/Friday

We found a US web belt with three frags and a trip flare on it. During the night we heard some heavy firing about seven hundred yards northwest of us. I got on the radio and was told it was a CCN recon team. I asked if we could help, but was told no. It lasted for quite a while.

21 February 1970/Saturday

Bates sighted ten gunkies to his northeast.

We went northwest up this hill in the direction of where the CCN recon team had made contact. We heard a lot of movement towards the top of the hill. We stopped at a creek and waited, but nothing happened. So we filled our canteens, cooled off a little, and began to hump. We got about twenty yards or so when we again heard movement. We stopped again and got down. Then one of the guys spotted a bunch of huge brown, black, and red monkeys in the trees! I never saw a monkey in the wilds before. They were pretty neat. They just sat there perched in the trees and watched us. We watched them for a little while then continued on. We went about a klick and found an NVA campsite next to where we will exfil. Since a landing zone was right next to us, we set up in the campsite. Was a little spooky because we knew the gunkies were in the area.

22 February 1970/Sunday

End of mission. The nighttime wasn't too bad. We heard some noise, but nothing happened.

Rose's recon team in contact. They got eight NVA. Chief Edwin (Lee) got his ruck shot off his back, and Masson (his second tour) got his poncho shot up while wearing it!

24 February 1970/Tuesday

Black's recon team set an ambush and got two NVA and a POW!

A bunch of us went to Eagle Beach today and raised hell with the civilians. We got an MP escort out of Hue on the way back. The commanding officer was pissed!

26 February 1970/Thursday

19th Mission–Anteater–XD3782

Lt. (Kevin) Henry, our cherry 2d Platoon leader, typical dumb-ass lieutenant, put us in the wrong area of operations. I figure we're about a klick from where we should be. But Lieutenant Henry says I'm wrong. I've been around for a little while and know my job. I really know how to read a map. I rarely even use my compass. That idiot! Lieutenant Ohle has left and Henry is taking his place. Henry is a nice guy, but not too smart. I guess like typical dumb-ass lieutenants, he can't stand to be wrong. Especially when it's a lowly corporal.

Bates exfilled Mannerburg because of injury.

27 February 1970/Friday

We can't get an azimuth because of the low clouds. But I really know where we are, and it isn't where we're supposed to be!

Bates exfilled Stauffer because of sickness.

Rodarte's recon team exfilled a man because of sickness.

01 March 1970/Sunday

Bates had to exfil Martin this AM because of sickness. We heard the slick that picked Stauffer up yesterday, and spotted the slick that took out Martin today, so we linked up with Bates today. We're on QL-9, the main road that runs east and west from Quang Tri into Laos. We found a huge ball of rice and a marijuana cigarette on the road today. We all moved into the old Khe Sanh ville (the village outside Khe Sanh combat base) and set up an ambush on the road. Fowler and I set up at the extreme east flank. During the night, we smelled gunkies, then saw flashlights in the trees on the hill east of us. Looked like someone was turning in for the night. We just might get lucky in the AM.

02 March 1970/Monday

We moved out of the ambush at 0800 and moved into the bush on the other side of the road to wait for our exfil at 1000. Fifteen minutes before the exfil, Burg and I were sitting by ourselves on the east perimeter, when Burg heard a noise on the road. I tried to get everybody quiet, as they were all bullshitting. I then spotted a gunky in a crouch on the road. I started to fire, but stupid-ass McElroy and Buehrig were in my line of fire, still bull-shitting! The gunky spotted them and ducked and ran back towards his buddies. Burg and I then opened up and I threw a frag, WIA two. One gunky returned fire, but no damage. The guys didn't even know what was going on! Twenty minutes later a LOH arrived and said we had one body off the side of the road, on the opposite side from our perimeter, and had four rucks out on the road.

Burg, Andy, Morrow, and I went out onto the road to get the rucks. Burg and Morrow took the two closest and returned to the perimeter. Andy went for the furthest ruck, so I stayed out on the road by a ruck to cover him.

I was standing over the ruck, looking off to the north-east, when Andy was putting on a pith helmet that was lying next to his ruck. Just as he was bringing the helmet to his head, the DEAD gunky fired at me, but the bullet hit Andy between the thumb and forefinger of his right hand, exiting out his wrist. The bullet caused Andy to flip right off his feet and onto his back. The concussion felt like somebody had hit me in the face with a very large pillow, making me go back a step. The bullet had torn through Andy's wrist and blew some flesh and blood on me. I opened up right away on full-auto, putting several bullets into the gunky. I watched as the gunky's shirt moved with each bullet that hit him. I then went to Andy and put a big bandage on his wrist to cover the wound.

I stayed on the road and covered Andy as he crawled back to the perimeter. While Andy was still on the road, we took fire from the northeast, and I returned fire and the gunky dashed. After Andy got into the perimeter, I grabbed all his gear and the two gunky rucks, and walked into the perimeter. Bates yelled at me to leave the gear, but if it got hairy, I didn't want the gunkies to get their gear back and Andy's too. The LOH returned and Morrow and I went back onto the road to cover as Andy loaded and exfilled.

The Blues arrived and we all began a search of the area. All of a sudden, the DEAD gunky threw a fragmentation grenade at the Blues and ran away! I couldn't believe it! We called him "Super Gunky." First Burg and I put some bullets in him, we threw a frag that blew him into a bomb crater, the LOH gunner fired some bullets into him, and I pumped some more bullets into him. But that gunky was still able to shoot Andy and throw a frag at the Blues, and still get away! I was mad at first because the gunky had shot Andy, who was my best friend.

After the gunky had tossed the frag, I knew where he was to get him, but Bates held me back and said let the Blues do it. But the gunky got away. By then I had a lot of respect for the gunky and just wanted to meet him. What he did took a lot of guts. That is one guy who really wanted to live and not go down alone. I hope I'm the same way if I get the snot shot out of me.

The rucks had a lot of papers and maps. The papers said that the gunkies were a Chinese engineer team that was checking out QL-9 for use. There were orders, clothes, diaries, and a better map of Khe Sanh than ours. The map had camps, routes, caches, and the location of my mission and Dotson's on 21 Jan. I wish I could have gotten a body now. If those stupid-asses would have quit goofing off and gotten serious, we would probably have gotten the whole team of Chinese, and Andy wouldn't have gotten hit.

Andy was in surgery for over three hours. He might not get full use of his last three fingers of his right hand. I hope Super Gunky made it okay after all that. But I seriously doubt it with all the bullets he took.

During Luchow's infil, the slick crashed and Keough got a real bad concussion and had to be medevacked to the hospital ship. He wasn't responding to anything.

04 March 1970

Andy is doing okay and will be going to Japland tomorrow, and then home. I'm really going to miss him. But at least he's going home alive. I don't know what I'd do if he or Burg were KIA. They are my best friends and I would die for them! Keough was sent home with major head injuries.

05 March 1970/Thursday

S.Sgt. Eanes' recon team was surrounded by gunkies with dogs. Eanes was E-and-Eing with dogs chasing him, so he was exfilled.

I'll be going out with Yeck and Moran tomorrow. Burg and I refused to go out with McElroy. He's too noisy, he freaks during contact, and can't walk quietly or talk on the radio. He couldn't even fire his rifle during the contact when Andy was hit.

06 March 1970/Friday

20th Mission–Bushmaster–XD4398

Kris is on this recon team and he said he is really looking forward to working with me. I really like Kris. He's from California too. Shortly after we left the landing zone, we spotted a really huge bird perched on a tree on the ridge to the E. It then took off and flapped its wings really slow, but each time the wings flapped, it sounded like a .22-cal. Really neat looking bird.

Dad's birthday (48).

09 March 1970/Monday

Rose's recon team in contact. KIA eight gunkies.

We followed a trail with fresh tracks leading into a gully. We came across a large spider web strung across the trail and wondered how long it took the spider to make it. This has been here for a while because there was a lot of dust on it. As we got into the valley, we all felt pretty uncomfortable, like something was going to happen if we continued. So we backed off. There were fresh gunky tracks.

10 March 1970/Tuesday

End of mission. Our mission was cut short because headquarters said there are far too many gunkies in our area of
operations for our little recon teams. So what? Aren't we
supposed to find them and check them out?

13 March 1970/Friday

21st Mission–Jupiter–YD3913

My recon patrol is back together, but with S.Sgt. Cox as team leader. We have Vestal and Ut with us. Ut is our KCS [Kit Carson Scout]. I liked Ut right off. He was with the VC for about seven years before being repatriated. Sgt. Solko was put into our area of operations and we were put into his. Forty-five minutes in, I smelled gunkies. I told Cox to call a Pink Team, but he didn't believe me. Vestal and Ut were walking point, because I'm ATL and am walking rear. But the smell was really strong, so I persisted, so Cox finally called. He then sent Vestal and Ut up ahead and they ran into a base camp. Ut opened up, KIA one with bullets to his face. The gunkies opened up, and Vestal took a bullet in the right hand. We E-and-E'd back towards the landing zone, when I spotted and KIA a gunky in a tree. We had walked right by him, about thirty yards away, and he didn't even see us. But I saw him on the way back and killed him.

We moved about thirty yards further and stopped to direct the gunbirds. We then began taking bullets and Vestal was hit again in the right shoulder. The bullet went right through the meaty part of his shoulder and exited. We then took in some RPGs (rocket-propelled grenades) and I took some small fragments in my upper right thigh. I then spotted gunkies moving around to our right, so we dashed to the landing zone, taking fire all the way, and right up until the slick exfilled us. The gunkies had surrounded the landing zone, but we got out without taking further hits. Vestal will be on convalescent leave for about thirty days. We only got two KIA, but the Cobras cleaned their clocks!

15 March 1970/Sunday

Yeck in contact, six (NVA) KIA.

I went to Eagle Beach and wreaked havoc all the way there and back. I'd brought a smoke grenade and tossed it into a fountain at the three-way intersection south of Hue. It looked really neat with the smoke billowing out of it. I threw a smoke grenade with a fifteen-second-delay fuse out in some rice paddies. It blew like a frag and scared the hell out of all of us, including some villagers running to it to see what we had discarded. I didn't know it would explode the way it did.

I forgot to mention about the last time we all went to the beach and Al Dubravo was with us. An old mamasan was whipping an ox that was plowing a field. Al wanted to check his sights on his CAR-15, so he sent bullets into the ox, dropping it. Mamasan didn't realize the ox was KIA and kept whipping it. When we came back from the beach, a bunch of kids were climbing all over the ox, playing on it. I felt sorry for the mamasan after, because that might have been her only means of support. I will make the smoke grenade in the fountain a habit. We again raised hell in Hue, and were again escorted out. The commanding officer was pissed and restricted us from going anywhere outside of Eagle! Rats!

...uthor in the briefing room at the L Company (Ranger) tactical operations center. October 1969.

Mission Bushmaster.
Sgt. John Yeck reading
a letter from home.

Mission Bushmaster.
Assistant team leader
Jim "Bugsy" Moran in
the foreground, with Joe
Kennedy behind him.

Left to right: Sgt. Herman Brown, Patton, S.Sgt. Riley Cox, and Sp4. Burgess Wetta relaxing after a patrol.

Left to right: Sgt. Steve Mannerburg, Sgt. Tom Horne, and Sgt. Dav Hazelton cleaning weapons after a patrol.

Second Platoon Sergeant SFC Troy Rocha.

Mission Puma.
Left to right: Sgt. Bruce
Bowlin, S.Sgt. McElroy,
Sgt. Frank Johnson, and
S.Sgt. Andy Ransom.

Mission Puma.
Sgt. Frank Johnson
and Sp4. Burgess Wetta
on the radio just before
spotting monkeys
overhead in the trees.

Mission Puma.
Sgt. Andy Ransom
returning from a recon.

Mission Puma.
Sgt. Frank Johnson
waits for the enemy.

Sgt. Fowler, with Sgt.
Rick Butler behind him,
before a mission.

Sgt. Rick Butler, with Arroyo in
background, before a mission.
Rick didn't smoke in the field.

Mission Anteater.
Third day in the bush.
Team leader S.Sgt. Jim "Lobo" Bates.

Mission Anteater. Fourth day.
Team set in ambush. Left to right:
Sgt. Fowler and Sgt. Frank
Johnson. A Chinese engineer
team was spotted bedding down
for the night in the trees
in the background.

Mission Anteater. Contact!
Sgt. Frank Johnson returning fire.

S.Sgt. Gary Sands and Sp4. Burgess Wetta in the company area after a mission.

Team 24 preparing for a mission. Left to right: Sgt. Vestal, Kit Carson Scout Ut, and S.Sgt. Gary Sands.

Mission Beetle. Left to right: S.Sgt. Gary Sands, Sgt. Vestal, Sgt. Bruce Bowlin, and Sgt. Fowler chowing down on papayas and sugar cane in the bush to celebrate Sands's birthday.

Mission Montana. Premission briefing at the company TOC. Left to right: Sgt. Arsenault, Sgt. Dave Casey, S.Sgt. Ray Ellis, and Sgt. John Beck. Ellis was killed in action during the mission.

Sgt. Frank Johnson in the company area.

Relaxing in the company area. Foreground, left to right: Sp4. Mark Martin, S.Sgt. Jim Bates, Sgt. Frank Johnson, Sgt. Dave Hazelton, and Sgt. Jim Rodarte. Background, left to right: Sp4. Beuhrig, Sgt. Dalton, Sp4. Paul "Blinky" Morgucz, and Sgt. George McDonnel.

Mission Grand Prix. Front row, left to right: Sgt. Rick Butler, Jim Dunkle, and our Kit Carson Scout. Back row, left to right: Sp4. Bo Clark and Sp4. Tuisee.

18 March 1970/Wednesday

Colonel Bindrop arrived and gave Sgt. Brown the award
for Soldier of the Month. Then he gave us a speech on the
great job we're doing. It was crap. Burg and I are going to
China Beach for three days on the 26th.

19 March 1970/Thursday

Was supposed to have gone out, but the area of operations is too socked in. There were three slicks with a recon team in each and two Cobras flying to the area of operations. When we turned around to come back, south of Firebase Bastogne, a gunky .51-cal. opened up on us. Missed by a mile, but what balls!!!

20 March 1970/Friday

22d Mission–Neptune–YD9957

Recon team #24 Phantom Rangers:

TL: S.Sgt. Cox
ATL: me
Radio: Burg
Jradio: Sgt. Bowland
SCT: Ut
RM: Sp4. Steijen

Steijen is taking Vestal's place till Vestal heals. We moved east, uphill, and found a very fresh set of gunky tracks and a gunky tennis shoe. We moved a little further and heard a lot of movement. So Cox decided to turn around and we went to the other side of the landing zone. About fifty yards past the landing zone, we again heard a lot of movement ahead. So Cox sent Steijen and Ut up ahead to recon. About fifty yards further, they ran into a base camp.

As they were coming back, two gunkies began walking in our direction. So Ut and Steijen opened up, KIA both. Then all hell broke loose. We took AK and RPG fire from the camp. Steijen had a bullet go right through his left breast pocket. The Cobras worked over the area while we beat feet back to the landing zone. The gunkies tried to flank us and a bullet went right through my right pants leg, just below the knee, that almost knocked me down. It felt like somebody tried to trip me. Bowland had a bullet go through his pants leg too. Bowland and I took cover on the other side of the landing zone, while the rest of the recon team stayed on their side. While we were being exfilled, the door gunner, Bowland, and I opened up on our side of the landing zone and heard screams.

Bates in contact, one KIA.

Moran's recon team is the only one left out and he's supposed to have the hot area of operations.

We were all joking about who was going to make contact this mission. Ours was supposed to be the cold area of operations but we made contact first and with the most gunkies. I like these one-day missions. For a while there I thought I wasn't going to see any action and wouldn't have any fun. I'd gone a long time without any contact since November. I've had some pretty good fights so far, but I hope this isn't all. S.Sgt. Solko went his whole tour without any contact, and not even a sighting! His closest contact was when I took the bullet in the chin.

23 March 1970/Monday

R&R in three days! We couldn't talk SFC Rocha into letting us go to China Beach early. We could've snuck out, but Burg gave us away by asking instead of just going. No one would have known, and no one would have said anything anyway. Oh well, what are friends for?

26 March 1970/Thursday

Left Eagle at 0830 by Chinook and arrived in China Beach at 0945. It was a very bad ride, too bumpy. This is a pretty nice place. There's a big club with a bar every night. Tonight is an Aussie band that is pretty good. No girls!

27 March 1970/Friday

This is pretty nice, but we should've gone to Saigon instead. There are no girls here. There is a village right outside the perimeter, but it's off limits. We could sneak in,
but Burg is married and won't go. I don't blame him
though. But I'd sure like to go. There is an outstanding
band tonight. It has two girls and one is a real clown.
When she dances, she looks like she has her feet nailed to
the floor, and she's trying to get loose but can't. It was
pretty funny. During the day, Burg and I went surfing and
played a little football. I can't surf to save my life.

28 March 1970/Saturday

Last day. It was fun, but no girls. I'm really relaxed. I guess I was wound tighter than I thought.

29 March 1970/Sunday

Spent six hours trying to catch a Chinook out, before we found out they don't fly on Sundays. We stayed at the Da Nang airport until 2030, until we caught a ride to Phu Bai. While at Da Nang airport these five American girls came walking through. Everybody in the place almost died. They were really beautiful, or it has just been a long time.

We met some guys from N Company, 75th Infantry (Ranger), with the 173d. I asked them about John Sherman, who I had gone through Recondo School with. They said John was KIA by several bullets to the body! I couldn't believe it. He was really a great guy. They said he really went down fighting, making the gunkies pay for his death. They had heard about our singing in the school and thought that it was pretty funny. I'll miss John. Burg and I got as far as Phu Bai tonight and spent the night.

30 March 1970/Monday

When we walked into the company area we were told that
we are going on a secret mission tomorrow. I have to wait
to say what it is, if I make it.

31 March 1970/Tuesday

23d Mission–North–YC387991

What a farce! We were broken into three forces of four teams each and were supposed to attack and blow up three bridges in the A Shau Valley. I led Team 3, the North Force. We were to provide security on the near left side of the bridge.

We went into the A Shau at 0700. As the first slick went in, the second slick's rotor struck the first slick's tail rotor and the first slick crashed. Kris was exiting the first slick as it crashed and was thrown out, then was hit in the head by a piece of the rotor and got a real bad concussion. We all took up positions around the downed slick, while Yeck took his team to recon the bridge. He discovered the bridge to be two slabs of PSP (perforated steel planking, used by the Air Force for quick-and-dirty runway construction) across a creek three feet wide! What a damn farce! When we got back to the company area, my recon team was rucking up to go out, so I rucked up and went. Burg tried to get me to stay, but my "mission blood" was running.

24th Mission–Tarantula–XD8538

I have a new team leader, S.Sgt. Gary Sands. Great guy. We are a stay-behind with A Troop, back in the Khe Sanh ville area of operations. As soon as we separated from A Troop, they found and KIA a gunky. On their way back to Quang Tri, one of their slicks was shot down while flying over the Rock Pile. When they landed they found an occupied cave. In the fight, they had one of their own KIA and five WIA. I don't know how many gunkies they got.

We found a fresh tunnel, and fifteen yards further on we heard gunkies talking in some real thick brush. I wanted to get them because, at the time, A Troop was still on the ground to reinforce us and take the bodies from us. But Sands didn't want to, so we bypassed them. I think we should have taken them!

01 April 1970/Wednesday

We found a bunch of fresh rest areas under the elephant grass. We set an ambush a hundred yards from where Andy was hit. Seems spooky to be here for some reason. I think it's because we let those gunkies go and we feel on edge because of it.

02 April 1970/Thursday

Ambush in vain. I think we're being followed. It's a sixth sense I've developed and it hasn't let me down yet. I'm sure God is looking out for me. We moved into the Khe Sanh ville. It's spooky knowing Andy was hit here. I've become very cautious this mission. I should have gone on R&R, or else gone out of country. It's been raining, so the water has washed away any sign of gunkies. The gunkies like to use this area of operations, so I know they are around. We set an ambush in one of the old houses in the ville in hopes of catching gunkies wanting to get out of the rain. I don't like it here.

03 April 1970/Friday

No visitors. We moved up the hill to check some old trench houses that still look intact. We found bats in one and I KIA a VC bat when it began flying around. We then moved west, across the river to QL-9, and set an ambush on the road. Hope this works.

04 April 1970/Saturday

End of mission. We had a really beautiful ambush, but again no visitors to share it with.

Eanes' recon team in contact with twenty gunkies carrying RPGs. Zentner WIA above the left eye and Eanes caught fragments in his face. The recon team got out and Eanes will be going home because of his wounds. Their KCS [Kit Carson Scout] KIA two gunkies.

06 April 1970/Monday

S.Sgt. Kline's recon team ran into a trail watcher and they fired him up.

There was a Korean show at the 501st Signal Battalion tonight and they had the three most beautiful Orientals I've seen in a while. One of the best shows I've seen too. Afterwards Bowlin and I went to Sands and Steijen's hootch and got plowed on scotch and coke. I passed out at about 2400, right outside the hootch, and Burg came and picked me up and carried me to our hootch and plopped me into my bunk. You know, he's just like a brother to me. I really love him. I've only got a few really good friends, guys I would die for: Ron Hamilton, Ted Robinson, Al Dave, Andy Ransom, and Burgess Wetta! I'm not much at making friends, but I really love these guys.

07 April 1970/Tuesday

Man am I ever sick! I can barely stand up. I almost
missed the AM formation. I crashed until about 1500, because I'm going out tomorrow. Wow, I've got to take it
easy, can't move real fast. Everything gives me a
headache today. I didn't eat until supper, and not much of
that. The area of operations we're going into tomorrow is
supposed to be real hot. It's supposed to be a base camp
area with a lot of gunkies. Maybe I'll run my KIA up. I
made Sgt. today for the second time! Maybe I can keep it
this time. My MOS (military operational specialty) is
now 11F4P (Combat Intell-ES-Paratrooper).

A couple of days after Andy was hit, Top took me to
an oral board made up of three officers and an NCO who
didn't know crap about LRRPs. But according to Top, I
devastated them with my knowledge and the courage
I showed. Top had really spoken up for me about the job I
have been doing since I've been with the Rangers.

08 April 1970/Wednesday

25th Mission—Grasshopper—XD9936

THE SHIT HIT THE FAN TODAY! We're heavy with Zentner's recon team (eleven of us). We came in on four slicks, with the last two being empty to make it appear we've got a lot of troops. The landing zone is on a finger where there is a freewaylike trail running the length of the finger, and a whole lot of trails run off this main trail.

I'm walking third behind Ut and Steijen, and am first off the first slick, with Ut right behind me. As soon as Ut and I hit the ground, we spotted a whole mess of gunkies to our east, running away from the landing zone, downhill. A LOH then spotted two gunkies on the trail above us. We waited ten minutes, then Ut, Steijen, and I went on a recon down the trail to the east, following the large group of gunkies. We went about one hundred yards when Ut spotted several gunkies ahead. Ut suspected a very large base camp was nearby. We returned to the recon team and then we all went back down the trail to hunt the gunkies. We knew this area was hot, so we were there only to hunt and kill.

We infilled at 1330, and about 1630 and 500 yards later, the slicks returned to fake an exfil. When the second slick lifted off and the first slick was circling away, the gunkies opened up on the slicks with .51-cal. from about seventy-five yards below us! The gunkies were laughing and moving uphill towards us, not knowing we were there. Blinston saw them first and opened up, killing one. The gunkies then rushed us. McSorely, Zentner with the M-60, and Blinston were the first to get rushed. Mac then grabbed the M-60 and killed two, then yelled at me and said, "Wow, I feel like John Wayne!" The gunkies were trying to flank us, but we put out too much fire. I used my M-79 (40mm single-shot grenade launcher, sort of like a huge single-barrel shotgun), shooting into the trees, to make the shrapnel spread more. It seemed to work pretty well; the gunkies quit trying to come around my side.

We couldn't get commo for the first twenty minutes, but finally got a Cobra. The Cobra then started firing for us, and radioed our contact. Lee then killed two gunkies. I then felt like getting down, as I always get up on my knees so I can see. I told Steijen we'd better get down, but he stayed up. An RPG then hit about ten yards in front of me and the fragments went flying right over me and Steijen took a hit in his left forearm. I laughed at him and told him he'd better listen to me next time. I then patched him up. Blinston then took a bullet in his left bicep, and Mac KIA the gunky who shot Blinston.

After about an hour of exchanging fire and frags back and forth, we grabbed our gear and moved back towards our landing zone. I stayed behind and set up a claymore/WP. Ut and Sands stayed with me to cover my rear. When the gunkies showed, I let one pass my claymore and blew it, killing about a dozen.

The recon team had moved about a hundred yards when Mac, walking point, ran into a force coming down the hill at us. He killed three, then his CAR jammed and he was sprayed across his chest. Mac was about ten yards ahead of the recon team and lay out in the open, still alive. Lee was then hit in the elbow, shattering it. Zentner opened up with the M-60, killing two.

Sands, Ut, and I returned to the recon team at that time, and heard what had happened. I was pissed because Mac's slackman should have been right behind him. Anyway, Mac was a good friend of mine. I started for the front, but Sands told me to stay there to protect our rear. He said he would get Mac. Sands then went up front and crawled the ten yards in the open, grabbed Mac, and dragged him back to the perimeter while under fire.

I could hear Mac scream when Sands was dragging him. I couldn't stand it and it made me real mad. I started to go up front, but Ut grabbed me and didn't want me to leave him by himself. So I stayed. Mac died fifteen minutes later!!! DAMN!!! The Cobras then gradually worked all around us and the fire died to our rear, then gradually died to our front. Sands came back to me and said it was like a circus. We'd fire, then the gunkies would fire. It was like two pop-up targets trying to shoot each other, but not wanting to get hit.

When it got dark, Spooky (aircraft specially fitted to drop flares) fired flares for us for about an hour, then quit. Sands went back up front while Ut and I stayed put. After Spooky quit firing flares, I crawled out about twenty feet and set up a claymore. About twenty minutes later, the gunkies came at us from the rear. I waited until they were right on my claymore, then blew it, killing five that I could see. The rest of the night the gunkies kept trying to move around us, but one of us would throw a frag or two. I killed five more, Ut got three or four, and Bow two.

All this time, two more .51-cals. opened up on the

slicks and Cobras from two other ridges. Twice a Medevac tried to exfil our killed and wounded, but the fire
was too heavy. One Medevac pilot was KIA, one WIA,
and one door gunner WIA.

09 April 1970/Thursday

Finally, at about 0020, two slicks came over us and one
dropped a jungle penetrator and exfilled Mac and Lee.
The other dropped a Maguire Rig and exfilled Steijen
and Blinston. I couldn't look at Mac. It made me cry to
see him. I should have been with him. His slackman
should have been right with him! At 0205, the rest of us
exfilled by ladder. Before Mac and Lee were exfilled,
Stinger fired for us in an attempt to get the gunkies to
back off for the exfiltrations. Stinger fired miniguns right
down on top of us. I was watching them fire when I saw a
burst exit the plane and make its arc right towards us. I
yelled for everybody to look out, and the bullets hit right
down the middle of our perimeter! The .50-cal. bullets
were so big that when they hit the ground, you could feel
the concussion of each bullet. I thought I was going to
get hit, so I curled up in as tight a ball as I could and just
tensed up, waiting for the impact. Man that was close!
The bullets actually hit three feet behind me! I don't
know how no one was hit. God was really looking out
for us!

By the time we exfilled, four Cobras and two slicks
had taken serious hits; Stinger was fired at; a pilot was
KIA; and three pilots and two door gunners WIA. The
fast movers are supposed to work over the area tonight
and a grunt unit is going in to sweep the area. We had to
leave our rucks, and I booby-trapped mine with frags. So
I told headquarters to let the grunts know so they don't
get whacked.

We got back at 0315, and the whole company was waiting for us on the pad. That's our company policy when any recon team gets in contact or even when they just return from a mission. It's really neat to have everybody greet you at the pad and help with the gear, and just to have somebody there.

When I got off the slick, Burg was there and grabbed me and gave me a great big bear hug. He was crying and said he thought it was me who had gotten hit in the elbow and refused medical attention, because he says I'm that stubborn. But I told him it was Lee, who is also that stubborn. We were then taken to the mess hall and fed steak and eggs.

I felt really bad about Mac, but that was the way he wanted to go, FIGHTING! And he definitely went down fighting. He was from Canada. He and I were talking about getting a mercenary team together after this was over and hire out. He had sent a complete CAR-15 home to his parents. The guys told me that when Burg found out I was in contact, he sat down in the tactical operation center crying and praying for me! You can't beat a friend like that! Thank you, Lord, for such a great friend!

We got twenty-seven guys from D Company, 75th Infantry (Ranger), from II Field Force when it was deactivated in April. I guess the war is winding down! Sgt. Robert Neal, who was with Bates and me in NCO school, was with II Field Force, and is now with us. It's good to see him again and have him with us. These guys have been working in grass and forests, not jungle. They've been fighting VC and not NVA. I think they are going to be in for quite a show. They might find the

NVA don't fool around like the VC do. The NVA don't run like the VC do, either. The NVA use tactics and signal with whistles and have a helluva lot more firepower than the VC.

10 April 1970/Friday

We had a memorial service for McSorely today, conducted by Chaplain Lord. It was a pitiful service! He was
telling us how David, of the Bible, would sometimes go
behind enemy lines and even into the enemy's tents. That
the men in those days were great athletes and ran great
distances. But that David prayed and the reason Mac died
was because he didn't pray. The chaplain said we don't
believe in God and we don't pray.

Damn, that made me mad! I yelled "Bull shit!" and
said I'm not listening to this crap! I then walked out of
the formation. Bates got in front of me and told me to
stay in the formation. I said no, that this turd doesn't
know us and doesn't know what we believe in. I then
walked out of the formation, turned to Captain Guy, and
said, "Sorry, Sir, but Mac was my friend and this bum
doesn't know us from the gunkies! I was there and we
were outnumbered and Mac saved us from getting shot
up worse than we were!" I then walked into the club.

The stinking biased turd! When I walked out, several
others followed. The commanding officer met me in the
club and apologized for the chaplain. I said I was sorry
for walking out. We all then had some beers on Mac!

Burg went out this afternoon with Yeck and hurt his back
during infiltration, while jumping from the slick. Damn it, I
knew something was going to happen to him. His back
bothered him in the formation today. He was taken to the
18th Surgical Hospital in Quang Tri. He originally injured
his back when he was quarterbacking in college.

11 April 1970/Saturday

I saw Burg at the hospital in Quang Tri. It was really sad. He's being doped up because of the pain. I wish I could do something for him.

Buehrig, on Yeck's recon team, put out his claymore and when he connected the clacker, it went off, blowing crap into his face. I guess it was pretty bad.

13 April 1970/Monday

We started toward our area of operations for our mission, when the fan that cools off the oil to the engine in the slick broke. We were forced to land in a valley northwest of Firebase Sarge. On the hill to the west a Pink Team spotted and fired up ten gunkies walking in our direction. They killed three of the ten. Then the Chinook that was taking out our downed slick took fire as it cleared the valley south of us. We went back to Quang Tri for the night because it was too late to infil somewhere else.

14 April 1970/Tuesday

This AM a LOH spotted six gunkies swimming across the river, pushing equipment on a raft. They KIA all six. A Troop went in and collected the bodies and gear. The gunkies had a complete map of Camp Carroll, showing weak points. One gunky was a captain and one a lieutenant.

26th Mission–Beetle–XD8237

We're west of the Khe Sanh ville. Sgt. Vestal is back with us and Fowler is taking Burg's place. Steijen is no longer going out because he's a short-timer now. I smelled gunkies during the night. I have a bad feeling.

15 April 1970/Wednesday

At 0900, a Pink Team took fire from a .51-cal., five klicks west of us. They then took fire from a bunker complex in the same area as the .51-cal.

This AM we found a gunky fire pit, but no recent use. This afternoon we found a campsite with a soybean-can wrapper that said "People's Republic of China." Ut said there were maybe three gunkies here in the last three days. Ut and Vestal went on a recon and brought back a bunch of sugarcane and papayas. They sure were good. This whole area is full of fruit. There is a road that runs next to this camp that shows use within the last twenty-four hours.

16 April 1970/Thursday

We did a pretty stupid thing. Ut climbed a seventy-five-foot coconut tree and threw down six coconuts. The tree was right in the middle of an open field. These guys have been too stinking noisy this mission, especially Vestal, Ut, and Fowler. Vestal is being an idiot and the others are following his lead. They want to make contact, but are being really stupid about it. I've survived so far because I'm careful, but these guys are going to get hurt, or get us all hurt. I have a feeling we're going to eat the big one. I'm surprised Sands is putting up with this. To top it off, we're having problems with our radio. One handset is bad and we've got a dead spare battery.

17 April 1970/Friday

Vestal and Ut were too damn noisy last night. They kept moving around and coughing like they were back in the rear. I smelled gunkies twice during the night. I finally told them what I thought about their actions on this mission, and that I smelled gunkies last night. That if I get hit because of their stupidity, I'm going to KIA them myself. They think I'm just being paranoid. I told them I've survived so far because of my gut feelings and because I'm careful, that they better knock off the crap. Vestal said I've had one too many contacts. I told him he will be the first one I KIA.

We moved to where we found the soybean wrapper to set an ambush at the campsite tonight. Everybody is being just too lax. Vestal got two papayas and we cut them into six sections and placed twenty-one matches into them, then whispered happy birthday to Sands, as it's his twenty-first birthday.

We were all relaxed and eating the papayas when I got this feeling to be alert. I told the guys, and sent Fowler to look down the road. Then we all smelled gunkies. Fowler went to the road and spotted two gunkies wearing khakis and carrying AKs. Sands got on the radio and said we are going to initiate contact. I was going to go with Ut and get the gunkies, but Vestal pushed past me and went. It made me mad, so I didn't go. They spotted the gunkies and opened up but missed, and Vestal's CAR-15 jammed! The gunkies immediately returned fire, then dashed when Sands and Fowler went to help.

I got on the radio and called in the contact. Vestal

couldn't get his CAR unjammed. We then dashed for a landing zone. A Pink Team arrived and worked the area over and we were pulled.

You know, these guys just don't know how lucky we are. I'm willing to bet the gunkies were planning on ambushing us. Thanks, Lord, for being with me and looking out for me! I love it in the bush and I love a good firefight. But I want it when I want it, and not when the gunkies want it. I love my job and am very good at it. But I'm good because regardless of how much I laugh and joke during the fight, the fight has always been in my favor, and not the gunkies'. That's why I have so much fun during the contacts. I know I'm going to win.

18 April 1970/Saturday

We got some ARVN Rangers in our company to work with us for a while. Burg got back from the hospital today. It's really sad to watch him and hear him talk. He's being kept doped up because of the pain and doesn't make a lot of sense. I should pay more attention to him. He's going to Hawaii on the 26th to spend R&R with his wife. It should do him good.

19 April 1970/Sunday

It was a pretty dull day until 2230. Burg, Cox, Bow, and I were in Burg's AO playing cards. Vestal, smoking MJ, got into a pissing contest with Burg. Burg made Vestal look pretty stupid and Vestal got pissed. He got his K-Bar and asked Burg how he would like nine inches of steel in his chest. Burg told him it wouldn't penetrate. They began arguing and Vestal got his CAR, stuck a magazine in it and put it on rock-n-roll. He pointed it at Burg's chest and said, "Let's see if eighteen rounds can penetrate."

Well, enough was enough, especially when it comes to Burg. So I stood up and told Vestal to quit playing the fool before someone gets hurt; and it won't be Burg or me. Vestal and I then got into some words. I finally told him to shoot, but he'd better KIA me right off because I'm going to KIA him. He backed off. He's an idiot! I should have KIA him and put him out of his misery.

21 April 1970/Tuesday

Hazelton took out four ARVNs and had two gunkies
moving towards him. So he set an ambush, but an ARVN
coughed and the gunkies beat feet!

Tonight, while Bow and Dalton were on bunker guard
(we have two bunkers to man on our perimeter), Vestal
and I went to the bunker and fired an M-79. The bunker
command post went into hysterics trying to find out who
shot the M-79. Vestal then got on the radio and told
bunker 13 to blow a claymore. When they did, the command post got really pissed and ordered whoever was im-
personating the command post to stop. Vestal and I went
to our hootch and fired a red pen flare into the air. The
whole bunker line thought it was an alert. It was pretty
funny.

22 April 1970/Wednesday

I got a military driver's license today. I'm twenty years old and I don't even have a civilian driver's license! I can drive anything from a jeep to a two-and-a-half-ton truck.

Horne's and Stauffer's recon teams came in early because of extreme heat. Broyles had heat stroke with a temperature of 108. I go out tomorrow.

23 April 1970/Thursday

It was 1330, and Sands, Rodarte, and I were waiting at Quang Tri to go on an aerial recon, when Hazelton's recon team had one, then two gunkies walk by his perimeter. He's got beaucoup signs of gunky activity all over his area of operations. Hazelton then had ten gunkies moving towards him, so he set an ambush. It was prematurely set off by one of the ARVNs with him. During the fight, Fowler was hit in the inside of his right thigh (his fourth Purple Heart) by a bullet.

A Troop was boarding slicks to reinforce Hazelton. Because all the slicks were now being used, we couldn't go on our aerial recon. Kris, Patton, and I were going to go with A Troop. But one of their lieutenants got really belligerent with us and said we couldn't go. I then got pissed and chambered a round in my CAR, and the lieutenant decided to let us go. We came in on a sandbar at the river and had to walk a ways to Hazelton's position. I walked point because the Blues weren't real enthusiastic.

After we linked with Haze, Fowler showed me his hole from the bullet in his leg. The bullet made a small hole and didn't penetrate through his leg. He was pretty proud of it since it was his fourth. Haze and two ARVNs went on a recon and got into a fight with five gunkies. Nobody moved to help, so I took off and Kris, Patton, Norton, and an ARVN followed me. The gunkies beat feet and we lost them.

We all then walked down to the river, with me at point again, ten yards ahead of the recon team. We were crossing a cleared-out area when some gunkies opened up on me from across the river. The bullets buzzed all around me, but not in me! I don't know how I didn't get hit! There is no feeling in the world like having the bullets flying around you! You can feel the concussion of them passing you and it just makes you move with each bullet that goes by. If there are several, then your body just moves all over until you finally get the strength to drop. and even when you drop, you can still feel the bullets above you.

The Cobras then worked the area. We all exfilled, but Haze's recon team stayed and set an ambush, hoping the gunkies might think everybody had left and they might catch them unawares. When I got back to Quang Tri, Sands told me I might get into trouble for going to Haze's aid.

24 April 1970/Friday

27th Mission—Alabama—YD0743

When we first went in, our KCS, Huan, wouldn't jump the six feet from the slick. So the door gunner kicked him out. It was pretty funny. Huan landed right on his face. Huan was a lieutenant with the NVA for thirteen years. I'd been on a mission with him on Dotson. Huan just wasn't used to the slicks yet. Dalton is now on my recon team and Huan is Dalton's KCS. So because Dalton went to the KCS school and got Huan, and Dalton is now on my recon team, Huan is also with us, and we lost Ut. I was pissed when I was told. I don't know Huan and don't trust him.

Ut and I had gotten pretty close. He had apologized to me for his actions on the last mission. He said he has a lot of respect for me because not only am I the most aggressive soldier he has seen in combat, but I see things nobody else sees. He says I see visions. I told him it was just God taking care of me. Ut and I had this contest to see who gets the first and who gets the most KIA. I'm not sure about the first, but I've got the most.

We found a trail junction marked with an X, which means a base camp nearby. But we couldn't find it. I smelled gunkies during the night. This morning Haze spotted two sampans on the river with a total of thirty gunkies. He called a Pink Team that sank the sampans. Rodarte, with a sniper rifle, and Morgucz, with an M-60, were infilled to reinforce Haze.

25 April 1970/Saturday

At 0400, Haze sprang his ambush, but Morgucz froze at the M-60. Martin was hit in the wrist. No KIA! Morgucz is a cherry. You can't blame just one guy for a blown ambush. There is a whole recon team with him who all have guns too.

Most of the humping for us was on our hands and knees. We finally got to a creek and followed it to QL-9, where we found tracks of three or four gunkies no more than twelve hours old. We set an ambush on the road. Huan doesn't read sign like Ut does. Ut has taught me well. I am able to read sign. Huan didn't even see the tracks.

26 April 1970/Sunday

We checked the road this AM and found a set of tiger tracks! I didn't sleep much because Huan wanted to pull guard last night and I don't trust him yet. We followed a creek bed until 1330, then stopped for a rest. All of a sudden we heard noise on the bank to the west, above us. It sounded like someone was walking on the bank, trying to get behind us. It moved around to our rear and down into the creek bed, then walked right at me, at rear security.

We all sat very quiet and I put my CAR on auto, waiting for the gunky to come through the bushes between us. I kept low and kept my CAR low, when all of a sudden a pig came through the brush! Damn pig saw me and beat feet in the opposite direction. It scared the crap out of me! I almost pissed my pants. My adrenaline was pumping a mile a minute.

We then walked out of the creek bed and walked to the river, which was on the opposite side of the river from where Haze's recon team is. I then turned on the radio to make commo (as I rarely walk with the radio on to save the battery and help with noise discipline), and headquarters told me we are supposed to exfil because the ARVN grunts are going to make a large sweep through this whole area. Ten minutes later, Huan runs up and says there was a gunky right behind this bush to the east of us, twenty yards away. Huan and Sands gave chase and ran to where there were fifteen gunkies camped. Sands heard them just in front of him, beating feet. Our slicks came in and we exfilled without any problems.

There is a rumor that I might get busted for going to Haze's aid. Oh well, I'd probably do it again. My recon team couldn't go out anyway until all the birds made it back. So I don't know what the problem is.

28 April 1970/Tuesday

Drove around all day to get parts for a jeep. It was a lot of fun.

Ut went to Mannerburg's recon team. I begged Rocha to give Dalton and Huan to Mannerburg and give me back Ut. I'll give one Dalton and one Huan for one Ut! Rocha said no. DAMN!!!

29 April 1970/Wednesday

Ut, with Mannerburg, spotted and fired up a gunky, but missed. Nobody else saw the gunky, so they're staying out.

01 May 1970/Friday

28th Mission–Connecticut–YC8972

We're heavy with Haze. I guess the commanding officer feels if I want to go help Haze so bad, I can just go out with him. As soon as I got off the slick, I found a well-used trail. We didn't cover much ground today because of the heat. We stopped on a peak that looks like a rest area on this trail. We set an ambush here.

We heard three bursts of auto fire that came from the gully to the north-northeast. We've been hearing movement to the north most of the afternoon. It's coming from the side of the hill we're on, like there is a trail that runs the side of the hill. The jungle is real thick, so we can't see very far.

02 May 1970/Saturday

We had a helluva hump today. The terrain doesn't coincide with the map. The map shows this to be a ridge, but it's a bunch of really steep hills. We set up our NDP just after noon because of the heat. It's a good spot anyway. Sands and Huan went on a recon to the river below us and picked up this frog that's bigger than any frog we have back in the World. It also has a very mean disposition. It barks, and sounds like a Chihuahua, and bites everything that comes near it. We caught a big black bird-catching jungle spider. We then made the frog bark. When the frog barked, it jumped at us and opened its mouth real wide. We flipped the spider into the frog's mouth and the frog bit down on the spider and the spider bit the frog on its side. The frog immediately let the spider go and barked for about twenty minutes. The frog was really noisy.

03 May 1970/Sunday

Last night, Eagle was hit with twenty-six rockets. My company's area was missed. The gunkies damaged three slicks and one Cobra.

We heard two pistol shots that came from our last NDP. The gunkies must be using the trail and we didn't cover our tracks very well. It would only be a matter of time, so we dashed down the hill to the river. There were no signs that we were being followed yet, so we set up an ambush. While setting out our claymores, Anderson, a cherry with Haze's recon team, found a lone bamboo pit viper near his claymore. So Haze KIA it. Anderson doesn't know anything yet. He's pretty much a country bumpkin, a little slow. Pit vipers usually travel in pairs, male and female. The pit viper is called the "two step" because that's how far you get before you die after being bit by one.

Sands and Haze then attempted to string a trip flare on our back trail, but it accidentally went off and burned for fifteen minutes. So we packed our trash and moved up-river into some real thick bush about fifty yards away. I washed my shirt in the river and it sure felt great.

04 May 1970/Monday

No activity last night. We moved across and then down the river at 0630. We found a five-hundred-pound bomb in the river, in good shape. The wires had been pulled though. We then spotted tracks of two gunkies walking down the river, in the same direction we are going. They don't seem to be in any hurry, so they don't know we are behind them. We walked to the river junction and set up our NDP. We will use the sandbar for our landing zone for tomorrow's exfil. Just before dark, we heard a lot of movement coming from the bushes across the river to the west of us. But we couldn't see anything.

Vannig's and Zentner's heavy recon team had five gunkies following them, so they set up a hasty ambush. They KIA three and both Vannig and Zen were WIA in the leg by shrapnel. Bowlin was WIA in the top of his shoulder, and Keough (back from medical leave after his concussion) was WIA in the hip. Keough will be taken back to the medical ship and back to Japland again. Some guys just attract the bullets and shrapnel.

05 May 1970/Tuesday

The Lord is really looking out for us. An hour before exfil, Sands and Haze threw two blocks of C-4 (plastique explosive) and eight frags into the river, trying to catch some fish. No fish, but ten minutes later and one hundred yards upriver, two gunkies wearing khakis and carrying big-ass rucks, crossed the river from north to south. That must have been the noise we heard last night as the gunkies were settling in to their NDP. As soon as they got across, four more crossed from south to north, with one gunky in the middle wearing a bandage around his head. When they got in the middle of the river, Sands and Haze opened up, WIA one. I emptied a magazine and then got out a full magazine of tracers and WIA two more. The gunkies then dashed.

The Blues infilled with a Tracker Team and we all crossed to where the gunkies were. I found a tripod in the river that is used as a direction finder for mortars. On the north side of the river was a large abandoned gunky bunker complex that was completely covered over by trees. Headquarters says the gunkies were part of those that rocketed Eagle last Sunday. I wish I could have gotten one of those rucks and a body. If I'd had more tracers, we could've had a KIA.

I didn't appreciate Haze. When I pulled out my tracers, Haze tried to get them from me. The stinking chump can't shoot anyway. The guy isn't close to having the

KIAs I've got. Anyway, I wouldn't have tried to grab the tracers from him if they were his. It was like two kids fighting over a toy that one kid had and the other kid wanted and tried to get! Pretty sad.

07 May 1970/Thursday

Dembroski's recon team in contact. They had three gunkies walk into their twelve-claymore ambush and only got one KIA! I think some of our recon teams are farces. Too many guys either get too excited or just plain freak when the bullets start flying.

D Troop is trying their luck at LRRP missions. One of their teams had movement tonight and got scared and called for reinforcements. So nine more troopers went out to them. Pitiful! And they talk bad about us! They said anyone could run LRRP missions, and they can't even last one night! I talk bad about our recon teams sometimes, but I would rather go out with anyone from my company than anyone from another company.

09 May 1970/Saturday

29th Mission—Montana—YC6888

SFC Rocha is with us. He's been riding us pretty hard because his wife and he aren't getting along very well. So he fears that we might hurt him out here in the bush. I've always really liked him, so he doesn't have to worry as long as I'm alive. I will take care of him. It has been a long time since he has been to the bush, and he's never been on a LRRP mission. So being out here with only five guys is pretty scary for him.

I'm walking point for the first time in a while. It feels good to be out front where I can see instead of the back where I only get to hear about what's going on. I found a trail with signs of two landing zone watchers that had just dashed as we infilled. So we moved about fifty yards in their direction and set up for a while to listen. We heard movement for about the first half hour. We then moved fifty yards further and set up an ambush on the trail.

Bates had gunkies walk right by him, but he wasn't ready to do them, so he let them go by.

At 1630, Rodarte had beaucoup movement, so a Pink Team fired up the area of operations and then pulled the recon team.

10 May 1970/Sunday

We moved out early and followed the trail until it came to a gully. We stopped the recon team halfway down the gully, and Sands and I went on a recon down the gully to a high-speed trail that ran through a small creek. In the mud were six sets of gunky tracks not more than two hours old.

We went south on the trail for about fifteen yards and found an "X" made of leaves, which means there is a camp or rest area ahead. We moved a little further, when I spotted some kind of animal running down the hill at us. I couldn't see what it was for the tall weeds, so we backed up to see what it was. All of a sudden we heard a splash of someone walking through the creek, between us and the gully where the recon team was. I turned and started to walk towards the noise.

As I was about six feet from the bend that turned to my left, I came face to face with a gunky! He had his AK at the ready but I opened up first. I went for his legs, trying to just wound him. But the gunky started to turn to run, so I brought my CAR up and put a bullet into his face. The gunky ran about ten yards and fell. I could hear him breathing, because he fell facedown into the creek and was sucking water into his mouth. He died as I walked up on him. The bullet hit him in the left cheek and blew out the back of his head. It was amazing that the gunky even got this far with his head blown open like it was. He had me dead to rights, but I guess it wasn't my time. I just wasn't ready to die and he was. Thank God that I was faster!

Sands said there was another gunky behind this guy, but I only saw the guy I KIA. The gunky was carrying a ruck. Inside the ruck were two pairs of black PJs, a girl's hanky, a bra, rice, and sandwich bags of MJ, heroin, and hash, a poncho, and two poncho liners.

We moved back to the landing zone and were reinforced with Rodarte's recon team and some Blues. Ut was with Rodarte. I grabbed him and showed him my AK. We all then went back down to the contact site, then south to where the camp was. The camp was the same camp we had found on the last mission. We had just come from the other direction this time. The Blues then left us, but Rodarte's recon team stayed with us. I think this area is too hot for our little recon team. But that is why Rodarte is with us. Rocha doesn't like this at all. I told him we'll be okay and I'll watch out for him. He isn't comforted. We then set up in a thick stand of bamboo near the trail, so we can monitor it during the night.

11 May 1970/Monday

I was pulling guard at 0430 this AM, when I heard auto weapons fire coming from Ellis' recon team area of operations. Then after a few minutes, I heard six single pistol shots. I tried to get Ellis' radio, but no one answered. I told HQ and they tried to get hold of Ellis' recon team, but couldn't.

SFC Taylor, the 1st Platoon sergeant, then grabbed a bunch of Rangers and infilled into Ellis' area of operations and discovered Ellis' whole recon team was KIA! Ellis had made his NDP on the top of a hill with a high-speed trail running right by him. Ellis was radio relay for the recon teams in the bush. Three gunkies walked up to his perimeter while the guards were asleep and KIA the whole recon team! SFC Taylor said he only found three piles of AK shells. Everybody was shot once in the head, and only the CARs and one radio were taken. That's why I always have two guys pulling radio watch and not just one.

SFC Taylor said he found Ellis' body outside the perimeter, as if he had woken up and tried to get away. The recon team never fired a shot! What a disaster!!! That is the danger of pulling relay, especially if there is only one hill to set up on. But you have to stay alert!

We had gunkies walking the trail during the night.

The trail was only fifteen yards away. At 1000, after SFC Taylor had found Ellis' recon team, Ut, Sands, Vestal, and I went on a recon, walking to the river to where we had made contact last mission. We ran into gunkies setting up an ambush. Ut and the gunkies saw each other at the same time, but the gunkies hesitated because they didn't see us behind Ut, and didn't know Ut was with us. Ut opened up first, but the gunkies returned fire immediately and Ut was hit in his calf. Another bullet went through Sands' right pants leg.

We all opened up and the gunkies dashed south and we dashed back to the recon team. A Pink Team worked over the area and Ut was medevacked. The Blues then came in and they all searched the area. They found a cave in the side of a hill to the west. I didn't go on the recon because Rocha was a bit scared, so I stayed back with him. We didn't find any more gunkies, so we exfilled.

Both Bates' and Lewis' recon teams had heavy movement, so they were both pulled.

Found out that Eagle had been hit by a 75 MPH typhoon, destroying a lot of hootches and buildings. My hootch held up though.

Lieutenant Colonel Molinelli came to our company today and we had a big bull session. We aired our grievances, and he gave his condolences for Ellis' recon team. It was a crock!

12 May 1970/Tuesday

Went to Eagle Beach today with a bunch of guys and raised hell coming and going. The water was great. Of all the people to meet, I met Mike Lindley! We grew up together from the third grade and had joined the Army together on the buddy system. But I had gotten separated from him at the end of AIT because I had caught pneumonia. He's been with the 2/327th Recon. We spent the whole day together.

He's lost a lot of weight and is having a hard time. His last time out, he was walking third in a four-man point team, ahead of his unit. They were crossing a depression and he was climbing out of the depression when they were ambushed. The first two guys were blown on top of him, knocking him back into the depression, with the bodies falling on top of him. The last guy was also KIA. The gunkies then came and searched the bodies, and Mike played dead! He stayed there until his unit reached him. He was medevacked out because of stress. He said that was the closest he had come to death. I talked with some of his buddies and they said they are taking care of him. He goes home in July. He broke down and cried on me! I didn't know what to do or say. I wish I could have him in my company until he DEROSes. But he has some really good friends. I pray he makes it home okay! It was really good to see him!

13 May 1970/Wednesday

Last night, Sontag was giving a class to some cherries at Phu Bai about our company. A bastard E-8 (master sergeant) walked by and said, "Well if it isn't the big bad Ranger. I guess he never told you about the whole Team getting wiped out by only three VC!" Sonny said he was so pissed, but just walked away. A lot of lifers (career soldiers—among LRRPs they have the reputation of being timid time servers) have gotten a kick out of our recon team being wiped out. They've been laughing and giving us a hard time ever since. So eighteen of us went to Sonny's class today. Not a single lifer even stepped out of his hootch the whole time we were there.

Then, later that afternoon, I was sitting in my jeep waiting for Neilson, at the medics. This smart-ass S-2 (Intelligence) puke pokes his head out of the door and says, "Hey, Ranger, do you know there's a war on?" I jumped out of the jeep and said I'll show you a war, and chased him inside the building. He didn't think I would chase him into the building, and I caught him just inside the door. As I grabbed him, a captain comes in and tells me to let him go and to get out. I told him to tell his REMFs to keep their mouths shut or I'll personally show them a war! And that if he or any of his REMFs had ever seen the bush, they wouldn't be talking the way they were. The captain told me to get out. As I let go of the REMF, he shoved my hand away, so I hit him in the face and just walked out. Stupid-ass people, I don't see them in the bush doing anything. Punk-ass REMFs anyway!

18 May 1970/Monday

A Cobra mistook Vance's recon team and fired on them, setting off some CS grenades (harmless but very effective "crowd dispersal" gas grenades). The recon team got the full force of the gas and was pulled. I just want to know how the Cobra spotted them, and why did the recon team get gassed? That should tell you how not to recon, and how not to set up CS grenades! Pretty sad!

Then HH tried to put my recon team in tonight because Vance was exfilled and because we couldn't be one recon team short in the bush! We didn't even know our area of operations. We weren't given a chance to look at a map or get any info on the area of operations. Captain Stowers, our new commanding officer, wouldn't speak up for us. So Lieutenant Ohle flew us out of sight of Eagle for a couple of hours, then brought us back saying we couldn't find our area of operations because of darkness.

So what are these clowns doing in S-2/S-3 (Intelligence and Operations)? So one recon team short in the bush is going to make a difference to this war? It seems that everybody is on us since we lost Ellis' recon team. This is really pitiful! We're under the charge of 2/17th CAV because we use their slicks, Cobras, and Blues. They don't like us much either.

I got a letter from my Dad today, and of all people, Pam Carter! This is the first time she has written me since I've been here. She still thinks we're going together. She must have been dumped by a boyfriend.

19 May 1970/Tuesday

30th Mission–Georgia–YC8295

This is my recon team now. We're heavy, with Vestal, who has his own recon team (scary). Sands left for the 2/502d because he can't take this small-unit stuff anymore. I think that when Ellis' recon team lost it, that had a real devastating effect on a lot of people, and Sands is one. I'm going to miss him. I thought we worked well together. I really liked him.

At the landing zone, Vestal wanted everybody out one door. So Lagodzinski, from the Trackers, was first out the door, with Vestal, Huan, Dalton, and me last. Ski tripped a booby trap and was blown about eight feet in the air, blowing the whole inside of both legs and crotch. The slick exfilled with Dalton and me still on. It took off so suddenly that I almost fell out. We went back to Eagle to rig a Maguire Rig, but a medevac was able to exfil the recon team. Ski died twenty minutes later. Vestal took it pretty hard because he and Ski had become good friends. The guys in Ski's unit said that Ski knew he was going to die, so he'd written his parents a letter and given his friends his stuff. It was really sad. Ski had done three tours in Vietnam! I guess you have to know your limitations. He was a good guy.

21 May 1970/Thursday

Dembroski's recon team was put into Vance's area of operations where Vannig had ambushed the five gunkies (04 May). Somehow they got off a booby-trapped landing zone without any trouble. They found a fresh rest area, so they're setting an ambush there.

Ut and his brother and his brother's wife came by the company today. It was great to see him. He told me he would be back as soon as he heals. We went into the NCO Club, next door to our company. There is this real pretty girl working there, and I asked Ut to give me something real nice to say to this girl in Vietnamese. So he does, and I say it to her. All of a sudden this girl gets this shocked look on her face, yells something at me, then goes to the bar and grabs a bottle of beer and flings it at me. I ducked and she begins to grab more bottles to fling at me, so I ran out the back door. Ut had taken off soon after, so I didn't get a chance to know what I told her. I'll kill Ut when I get him!

22 May 1970/Friday

Late this afternoon a company of gunkies stopped to take a break at the rest area, in Dembroski's ambush. The recon team blew their claymores and KIA only two! The gunkies opened up and KIA Donahue with an RPG. Then Pretoric took a bullet in his left side.

It took the Blues a long time to get to the recon team, they were so scared to move. The Blues were even too scared to walk point back to the landing zone, and wouldn't help carry the casualties. So the recon team carried their own casualties and walked point! Pretty stinking sorry! This is the second time Dembroski has sprung a claymore ambush where he had a large force and the upper hand and came out the loser. He's from the II Field Force Rangers and not used to fighting NVA in mountainous terrain with thick jungle. He needs to be taught how to lay and set off ambushes so they work. So who's sorrier, Ski for not devastating the gunkies, or the Blues for being so scared? At least Ski is out doing it!

Rodarte has a lot of gunkies with flashlights moving around him.

23 May 1970/Saturday

Rodarte was pulled and placed into another area of operations. He made contact when he infilled into his new
area of operations, but the Blues were with him. The
Blues are staying the night with Rodarte on the landing
zone! Pretty stupid. Haze infilled today and began having
a lot of movement with gunkies using dogs. So we came
up with our own reaction force of eighteen guys divided
into three teams to rescue him. I'm ATL of A Team, the
point team. We were circling above Haze's area of operations when a Cobra went down in a rice paddy one mile
north of Hue. So we were sent there to pull security on
the Cobra until it was taken out, and Haze was exfilled.
What a rip!

25 May 1970/Monday

Haze went in yesterday and was going to stay at his NDP another night. But he thought better of it, and moved a hundred yards away. That PM the gunkies didn't know he had moved, and hit the old NDP with frags, satchel charges, and AKs. He's now got movement all around him.

26 May 1970/Tuesday

Haze made contact at 0400 and was pulled. When he got back to the company, a snot-nosed captain from headquarters didn't believe Haze had been in contact. So Captain Stowers took Haze and some Blues and the snot-nosed captain back into Haze's area of operations. Haze showed them his old NDP, where they found AK shells and frag holes. Then Haze showed them his new NDP, where they found AK and M-16 shells, frag holes, and two blood trails! Shut that snot-nosed captain up! It was probably that same captain that I had a run-in with when I hit that REMF. I was proud of Captain Stowers for sticking up for us like that. Capt Stowers said that because of Ellis' recon team eating it, that we are really being scrutinized for what we do. That we have to be really careful what we do and what we report. Not to exaggerate anything.

27 May 1970/Wednesday

31st Mission–Missouri–YC7395

Heavy, with S.Sgt. Rowles' recon team. We went in with
the Blues. We went about four hundred yards, then the
Blues backtracked and exfilled while we stayed in. There
is this big trail right off the landing zone, so we set an
ambush on it. It rained for about half an hour this afternoon. During the night, we spotted gunkies on the hill
above us with flashlights. I know they know we are here,
but they don't know exactly where. They stayed there for
quite a while, right above where we were, talking. I wish
Ut was with us so he could tell us what they were saying.
It looked like only four gunkies.

Ron Hamilton's birthday (20) [a friend from home].

28 May 1970/Thursday

We were going to stay put and attempt another ambush but our radio relay was pulled. So we had to move to higher ground for commo. We moved to the top of the hill we were on, where the gunkies were last night. When we got to the top, we were told that Rowles had to exfil because his mom is dying. So he gets to go home. We escorted him to the landing zone then returned to the top of the hill. We didn't have commo for over two hours. We finally made commo with a jet with our URC-10 and he relayed for us. We said we had movement, to speed things up and maybe get us exfilled and put into an area of operations with commo. But a Pink Team was sent out and they shot up the AO! Now we have to stay here after all this noise! This is great. Now we've really got ourselves in trouble. The gunkies already know we're here because of the four last night, Rowles gets exfilled, the jet gave our position in the clear, the Pink Team shot up our area of operations, and I told Henry that we are on the highest possible hill we can find to get commo! I feel like a damn cherry!

29 May 1970/Friday

We didn't have commo this AM and we had artillery rounds walked in to within two hundred yards of us. I got another jet on the URC-10 who finally got commo for us. I asked if anyone was firing artillery in our area of operations because we just had four rounds within two hundred yards. I was told no and to stay put. Then two recon teams infilled near the A Shau Valley with no commo. Henry said he is trying to get us pulled. But instead, a fixed wing was brought out to fly over each recon team's area of operations during the night for commo. We are supposed to check in at certain times during the night when the fixed wing comes over.

Delaney's recon team spotted three gunkies, so a Pink Team fired the gunkies up, but missed! Delaney was left out.

30 May 1970/Saturday

We were exfilled at 0800 and taken to Firebase Birmingham. There we were given orders to be taken to abandoned Firebase Whip, where we will be radio relay for Vestal's and Delaney's recon teams near the A Shau. Whip has no cover except three to four feet of scrub brush on the slope between the two levels. So we did the best we could. The firebase is shoe-shaped, like a quarter-high boot with two levels.

The east side of the firebase is a sheer drop. But the west side has a lower level. We set up in old bunker holes, minus the overhead cover, with just the scrub brush as cover. We stayed mainly towards the top of the firebase, overlooking the bottom level. Thirty minutes in, I got a call from headquarters, who said for us to make the best 360-degree perimeter we can make, that they can't tell me why on the radio.

Well, because of the way things were going for us and for our company, we figured these were probably our last days alive. So we began clowning around and making jokes. I was sharing a spot with Bowlin, who has been with me for quite a while now. I explained to him how we were going to get it, that the gunkies know we are here so the first thing that's going to happen is we get mortared. Then we get machine gunned. Then all we're going to hear, if we're still alive, is a bunch of yelling and screaming, and the gunkies are going to try to remove those of us who are left alive from this firebase, just like in the Korean War. Bowlin didn't like my humor.

I received a call from Vestal 2½ minutes later, giving

me his location. I radioed it in, then stood up and was taking an azimuth to see where he was from us. All of a sudden I heard gunkies talking and laughing! I got down and spotted two gunkies walking towards us, on the lower shelf of the firebase. I thought they might be a point to a larger unit. I told Bow, "Here we go!" I called in saying, "We have two gunkies coming towards us. It might be a point for a larger unit. I'm going to initiate contact . . . right . . . now!" At that time the gunkies were about forty yards away, walking parallel to me. I flipped my CAR to semi, stood up, and opened up, KIA one and WIA the other, shooting with only one hand, because I was still holding the radio in my left hand.

The WIA gunky ducked behind some stacked logs. The guys threw three frags, and I yelled for him to surrender. The gunky then started running back the way he came. He got about sixty yards when I put three bullets right in the middle of his back while still holding the radio in my left hand. I had tracers, so everybody watched as the tracers hit the gunky, knocking him forward onto his face. Everybody yelled in triumph over the shooting. Krause and a tracker went with us down to the bodies. They said I blew out the gunky's heart!

We were pulled twenty minutes later. When we got back to the company, I got a hero's welcome for some reason and a big hug from Burg. We found out that the warning we were given was because there was a battalion or a regimental NVA base camp at the base of the hill we were on. Bowland was pretty scared. He didn't fire a shot or throw a frag. He just stayed hidden. I didn't help matters much when I described how we'd eat the big one. He didn't like my humor. I don't know why, because he has been with me since January. He sticks to me like a leech every time we go to the bush. I don't think he's going to make it much longer. I really like Bow a lot, but his attitude has been changing ever since the Grasshopper mission.

Delaney had movement shortly after our contact, so he and Vestal's recon teams were pulled.

31 May 1970/Sunday

We found out (today) that those two gunkies I KIA yesterday were two of the three that wiped out Ellis' recon team. A diary was found on each of them describing the whole thing, even with a drawing. Two down and one to go. That was quite a psychological victory for us. It will make the gunkies think we are looking specifically for them, and have the capabilities to find the guys involved because we KIA two of the three. GOOD JOB!!!

Vestal was sent out again, but this time he's heavy, with S.Sgt. Norton's recon team. Kristiansen, Buehrig, and Huan were on a recon and ran into six gunkies. Huan was WIA in the finger, Buehrig in the arm, Dalton in the back and side by shrapnel, and Anderson burnt his hand by grabbing the barrel of his CAR. The gunkies got away!

03 June 1970/Wednesday

Moran went out today with six cherries (eight men). He spotted forty gunkies moving towards him. The gunkies were reconning by fire, so they were pulled.

04 June 1970/Thursday

I volunteered for radio relay and was put on Firebase Veghel, just east of the A Shau. It just reopened three weeks ago. They expect to get hit in the near future. I hope I'm here when it happens. I would like to experience it. The country is really beautiful here. I wish I could get a bow and some arrows and go hunting. I'm with Ballou and Devine. All we have to sleep on are two cots in a tent made of two ponchos. It rains every afternoon at about 1800, for a half hour each time.

05 June 1970/Friday

At 1830, Vance's recon team made contact with three gunkies. He was setting up his NDP, and they were putting out their claymores when the gunkies apparently spotted them and opened up on them. Bowlin was hit in the shoulder and a cherry in the chest. No gunky KIA! The Blues went in and they are all spending the night in a big ambush.

06 June 1970/Saturday

At 0845, Rodarte and Vestal's heavy recon team were being infilled by ladder. The slick took a sudden uplift, knocking the guys off the ladder from about ten or fifteen feet up. The second slick did the same. Rodarte broke open his head and broke some ribs and sprained his back; Vestal broke his leg and sprained his neck real bad; Anderson broke his hand; and Silva broke his arm. They were all taken to the 85th Evac. Rodarte lost consciousness twice en route.

Ballou and I went swimming in the little river at the bottom of the firebase this afternoon. We met Kellenburg from D Troop, who came by in a convoy. Kell used to be with I Company, 75th Infantry (Ranger), and wanted to join us (L Company), but Captain Stowers wouldn't let him because he's not jump qualified! Kell is really a good guy. He is Ranger School qualified, just never went to Jump School. I don't know what the difference is. It isn't like we make jump insertions. We could use Rangers, guys who have gone through the school to be LRRPs. Who cares if they can't jump?

09 June 1970/Tuesday

At 2010, Dunkle's recon team had heavy movement. He's surrounded by gunkies, but the gunkies don't know where he's at. The gunkies got within about fifteen yards, trying to find his claymores. The commanding officer said that if the gunkies find his claymores to blow them away. But if not, and Dunkle lasts until tomorrow, he'll be pulled.

10 June 1970/Wednesday

The KCS for Dunkle spotted a major among the gunkies this AM. A LOH flew over and spotted a bunker complex and then spotted three gunkies, so the LOH fired them up. Dunkle then dashed for a landing zone and was exfilled.

Sands came to Veghel today. He's with the 2/502d as a platoon sergeant. He has convoy security duty today. It was good to see him. I thought he was a good team leader and I miss him. But he just got scared working on such small teams so he transferred out.

I gave him the poop on my recon team. Burg hurt his back and probably won't be going out again; Bowlin transferred out also; and Ut was WIA. I'm the only one left on my recon team. Vestal has his own recon team, and I won't work with him because he's too stupid and dangerous. So until the commanding officer gets some more guys, I'm pulling radio relay. Anyway, it's a good break in the action. Bowlin went to Camp Carroll as an instructor to cherries. I wish him luck! We had some really great times together!

12 June 1970/Friday

This AM, Kline's recon team had gunkies firing mortars at him. They only got within about two hundred yards. He got a Pink Team to check the AO, and then Kline called in his own artillery. He called for an exfil because he can't move with all of the equipment they have. He has his recon team's gear, plus what the Blues left when they exfilled. They're stuck on their landing zone. He expects to get hit because they had taken mortar fire, and he'd been spotted earlier this AM.

But XXIV Corps HH said to stay put or pick up what he can and move. He's to blow in place what he can't carry with him. But Kline refused, so XXIV Corps HH said they would have a slick come in and the recon team will put the excess equipment on it. Kline said that if a slick lands, his recon team is getting on it. After about a half hour, Kline agreed to stay, but warned XXIV Corps HH to have body bags ready to pick up the KIA. Kline is right though. We aren't grunts to be left holding ground. The gunkies know he's there and the recon team isn't equipped to sustain a very large battle. We don't have the manpower or the weapons to hold ground. If XXIV Corps HH wants a pitched battle, then let them replace the recon team with some Blues or grunts. That's what they are for. You don't waste people like us on this kind of crap. We're an elite unit that sneaks and peeks on the enemy and fights the enemy on our own ground and when we want to, not vice versa. There are very few people who can do what we do. That has already been proven several times since I've been in this unit. I did a lot of talking with XXIV Corps HH in support of Kline. I think I'm in trouble for it. But the commanding officer won't speak up for us. I'm not making very many friends here. XXIV Corps HH finally agreed to pull the recon team. They were pulled this PM.

13 June 1970/Saturday

I returned to the company today. We're working Khe
Sanh and north of it. Haze made contact in the ville
where Andy was hit last March. They KIA one of three
and had to stay because the whole area of operations is
socked in. It has been raining like a son-of-a-gun. I'm
going out with Dunkle in a couple of days because he has
a whole recon team of cherries. I had felt like I was letting the guys down by working radio relay. Anyway, the
gunkies aren't going to hit Veghel.

15 June 1970/Monday

33d Mission—Grand Prix—XD8337

Infilled at 1730. We spent the whole day at Quang Tri waiting for the weather to clear. I met a really pretty girl who says she remembers me from the last time we staged out of Quang Tri. She thinks I'm cute. It's too bad I don't have more time before I have to go out. When we infilled, we walked about seventy-five yards north of the landing zone, then twenty-five yards back and set up an NDP ten yards into the bush. We've got an out-of-sight NDP.

I'm surprised how good I feel out here. I felt kind of scared returning back to the bush after being away for so long. I don't mind the contacts, but I hate the nights and being with stupid people. It seems that my last few recon teams have been with stupid people. This recon team isn't one of the better ones I've been with either. They are pretty sloppy. We are going to have to spend more time training them before they come out to the bush. I'll see what I can do.

At 2100, Zen's recon team made contact just a klick away with a hell of a lot of gunkies. McNabb got shrapnel in his foot and a concussion from a claymore blast. I wanted to help, but not a chance.

16 June 1970/Tuesday

Hund spotted five gunkies watching his recon team infil yesterday. One had an RPG. The Blues joined him for a while today, then left.

It's a lazy day for us. We can't move too much because Butler landed on Dunkle's ankle during our infil. Carter and I went on a recon and found an old bunker complex. No sign of recent use though. Carter is a very tall black guy. I tried to work with him a bit and show him some things.

17 June 1970/Wednesday

Uneventful day. Dunkle thought we had movement last night. I don't know how, he wasn't awake for very long. This AM Butler and Carter went on a recon and found an old grease gun (a World War II–era short-barreled submachine gun that fired .45-cal. ammunition that was unsuitable for work in Vietnamese climate; it quickly rusted). Colonel Molinelli flew over us and we took a fix from him because we're a little disoriented with all of the elephant grass (which was so high it made it hard to find a point of reference on a map).

I've been able to do a lot of thinking on this mission. I had been pretty cranky while in the bush and it's because we have had a lot of new guys who aren't trained right or just don't care. Either way, they aren't being taught to be professional. This isn't a game out here. The guys have been far too noisy and undisciplined. Some of the old foul dudes are becoming too lax, like Dunkle. Nobody stays awake during their watch at night. I've always had the upper hand out here because I've disciplined myself to sleep very little and very light. I've learned to catnap. Too many recon teams are being ambushed and losing their firefights. They aren't being effective. My recon teams have always had a pretty high KIA ratio. A lot of the recon teams are just plain lucky. They're lucky if they only get one KIA or none of their guys get hit. I guess the Lord is really watching out for us. Because that's the only reason I can think of why some of these recon teams are surviving.

Vance had seven gunkies five yards from his NDP.

18 June 1970/Thursday

Hund found a hootch with ten gunkies occupying it.
There is a sensor fifteen hundred meters from Hund that
reported twenty gunkies moving in his direction.

19 June 1970/Friday

We didn't get exfilled until 1400. We had to stay at Quang Tri until 2000 because all the slicks were being used. A LOH had found a very large gunky base camp in the foothills south of the Khe Sanh plains. Cobras worked over the area, then the Blues (ninety-five men) from D Troop were dropped in. They immediately got surrounded on three sides. All kinds of gunky equipment was captured from the base camp, especially papers. The equipment is really neat. They spread the equipment out for all to see at Quang Tri. A lot of magazines and grenades.

When we got to the company, we found out that the First Pig (company first sergeant) is kicking out six guys because they missed a formation!!! The commanding officer and First Pig are really stupid. The commanding officer kicked Rocha out because he said Rocha wasn't proficient anymore! You talk about chickenshit people! The commanding officer and First Pig want to get rid of the people on profile (light duty to recuperate) for longer than five days, and us old dudes that have been around for a while. They say we are too much of an influence and they can't run the company with us here. I really don't like the commanding officer and First Pig. A lot of guys are getting pretty pissed.

20 June 1970/Saturday

The *Hoc Bao*s came to our company today. They are an ARVN unit made up of convicts and criminals. *Hoc Bao* means Black Panther. They work in platoon-sized units. Ten of our guys are going out with them, and Moran wanted me to go with him. But I'd already planned a four-day R&R at Eagle Beach. So I declined. A big mistake.

21 June 1970/Sunday

(Rick) Butler and I are on our second of four days' leave here at Eagle Beach. There is a really good band here tonight. We had a good day playing tennis (which neither of us can play). We played pool and swam. Butler is kind of a dud though. Acts very young.

22 June 1970/Monday

Butler and I got a massage, but my girl didn't like me because I wouldn't tip her. To make matters worse with the girls, we threw one of the girls into the ocean with all her clothes on. Now we have all of the girls mad at us. Tonight Butler and I almost got into a big fight with B Company, 2/502d. They were on stand-down and were bragging about being the best unit in the 101st. So, like the good Rangers we are, I said the only real unit is the Rangers. It didn't go over very well with them. So we spent over an hour arguing, bragging, and threatening. It was a lot of fun.

Butler was scared because we were pretty well outnumbered, and he kept trying to get me to stop before we got our butts kicked. But I told him I hadn't been in a gang fight in a long time, and that all you have to do is hit the face in front of you. I told him to just watch my back. Nothing happened though and we all parted friends and had a great time.

23 June 1970/Tuesday

We returned to the company today and found out the ten guys that went out with the *Hoc Bao*s were still out. They were supposed to be gone for only a day to rummage around the gunky base camp area in the hills south of the Khe Sanh. Damn, makes me mad now that I didn't go with Moran.

24 June 1970/Wednesday

We got twenty-four guys together to go to Quang Tri to-morrow as a reaction force to bail out D Troop, who are in the base camp area in the Khe Sanh hills. Now maybe we'll get to show them how it's done. My recon team consists of: Team Leader, me; Assistant Team Leader, Butler; Carter, Cadena, Tuisee, and Brown.

25 June 1970/Thursday

The reaction force was called off. The ten guys with the *Hoc Bao*s returned today. They alone captured forty-four tons of rice, three base camps, and KIA three battalions of gunkies! They got enough documents to ruin the gunkies for months. It was a very big victory for our side, especially the *Hoc Bao*s. It makes me mad I didn't go with Moran.

Moran said the *Hoc Bao*s are really good and really take care of the Americans. He said as the *Hoc Bao*s prepared to attack a base camp, they would all get on line, jump up, and yell *"Hoc Bao,"* and then charge into the camp shooting and yelling. He said it was pretty funny. He said they go through the bush as quiet as we do with our small recon teams. Every night they dig bunkers for their NDP. Moran said they fix a hot meal every night, and that there is one guy who stays with you and does everything for you. All he did was sit back and watch. Moran said he had a great time. DAMN!!!

First Pig called in the MPs to take Krause and Super Nut out of the company area today. They were two of the guys that had been kicked out last week. They both had been back here since Sunday raising hell with the First Pig. The MPs finally got them after a lot of harassing from the rest of us. I don't understand what's going on here. It seems our company is falling apart. I think the commanding officer and First Pig are really tearing us all down.

26 June 1970/Friday

At 0200, nine of us hog-tied this cherry named Miller who had stolen Mannerburg's thirty-round magazine (bought from a catalog in the States; we only had twenty-round magazines!). We really did a job on him. Sontag and I cut big patches of hair from his head, then ripped open his shirt and put cammy stick, LSA, shaving cream, and dirt all over him. We then put him on the First Pig's steps with a sign that read, "I am a boy thief." The First Pig is kicking him out tomorrow. When Miller got here, he had a 201 file that read that this is his third tour. That he has been to Ranger, Jump, and Jungle schools. And that he has been WIA six times and has won a number of medals for valor. Apparently, Miller exchanged his 201 file with a guy who had the same name while at P Training. He's gone! Rangers don't steal from Rangers!

At 0315, Eagle was hit by rockets. It was pretty cool. I sat on top of my bunker at my hootch and watched the gunkies firing from two positions below Nui Kai Mountain. Four rounds came within a hundred yards of my hootch. There were three KIA and eight WIA from the 801st (a maintenance battalion). The fire was mainly directed at the CID and the MPs, but missed. It was a great show put on by the Cobras and Spooky, who were firing on the gunky positions.

Because of all the action in the Khe Sanh area of operations, I had suggested a POW snatch with Sonny,

Moran, me, Ut, Huan, and Lan. I was told it was a good idea and that we could probably pull it off. But we'll see what happens. Every time we plan on something neat, it ends up being just a dud or is called off.

28 June 1970/Sunday

The POW snatch is a no-go! So Ut and I went to the main PX and I stole a jeep. Ut and I then drove all the way to Quang Tri to his brother's house. You talk about a long trip! I've only been to Quang Tri by Huey, which only takes a short time. It took us almost all day. Going through Hue was the worst. There were people and vehicles all over the place. It was a little spooky being out here like this, but it was really fun.

30 June 1970/Tuesday

Ut and I got back to Eagle today. What a trip. I really had a great time. I loved it in Quang Tri. I have only seen it from the air, but it was nothing like being there. I loved the people and the smells. Ut's brother invited us back when we get the chance.

Burg told me that we're having racial problems. JC has picked fights with Butler and Haines. We never had problems until SFC Sanford got here. When JC was pulled off Butler, Sanford said for Butler to get all his Whitey friends and he'll get all his Black friends. If Sanford messes with me or Burg, I'll KIA him! Sanford is a commo puke. I really like our commo guys, but Sanford is a punk who's afraid of the bush. He thinks his crap don't stink. This was a really good company until Captain Stowers and First Sergeant Unzicker got here. And now Sanford. To top all this off, SFC Dobbs has replaced Rocha. Dobbs drinks a lot. Tonight he passed out standing up in front of my hootch. Burg and Dalton took him to his own hootch. I would have let him be. This is really pitiful!

The only good thing is that Lieutenant Ohle returned from his extension leave and is now a captain. He says he wants to be commanding officer of Company L.

01 July 1970/Wednesday

Today I went to Firebase Anne as radio relay. I had volunteered for Sniper School, so will be here until the 11th. Lieutenant Henry had stepped on his meat again. He was supposed to give our radio relays and the artillery people preplots and overlays of the three recon teams in the bush. But he said he was out of fuel and had to turn back. The commanding officer should've jumped dead on his butt and straightened him out!

02 July 1970/Thursday

Busy day. Norton's recon team has heard wood chopping all day, and they heard some voices sixty yards away. They can't use artillery because Henry STILL hasn't given the artillery people the preplots and overlays, or even the list of the recon teams in the field!

Rodarte spotted four gunkies about five hundred meters away. He couldn't get a Pink Team out because they are all on emergency standby only. A lot of slicks have been shot up lately. A Pink Team was in Norton's area of operations and spotted and shot at some gunkies, but missed them.

Rodarte then had movement between him and a river, so he dashed. He crossed a lot of fresh trails and found an eight-man sleeping position, so he's setting an ambush there.

03 July 1970/Friday

At 0300, Rodarte had five mortar rounds land within one hundred meters of his NDP. They landed about where his last NDP was. Then at 0320, the gunkies attacked his last NDP. Later this AM, two gunkies walked up to his present NDP and the recon team WIA one, but they got away. His recon team was exfilled an hour later. He should've had a Pink Team out there with him, but he was told his contact wasn't BIG enough! This is getting bad! I guess the mortars didn't mean anything!

When Rodarte made contact, the gunkies near Norton's recon team began yelling and screaming. At 0900, one of Norton's claymores accidentally went off so they had to beat feet.

JC, on Vannig's recon team, was bitten on the arm by some bug and his whole arm swelled up. He was exfilled.

06 July 1970/Monday

At 1520, Zentner's and Moran's heavy recon team (eight) infilled. Right off their landing zone they ran into about forty gunkies set up in a bunker complex. The recon team opened up and all hell broke loose. The gunkies opened up with AKs, RPGs, and .30-cals. Fifteen minutes into the fight, a grenade was thrown by the gunkies and landed at Kristiansen's feet and blew shrapnel into his legs and chest. Despite all the fire, Major Smith dropped in with his LOH and pulled Kris out and flew him to the 18th Surgical in Quang Tri. Major Smith saved Kris' life! A minute later, Neto was hit by shrapnel above his right eye. Zen was then hit in the arm, face, and stomach by shrapnel. The Cobras were working out like a son-of-a-gun, but it seemed to not work.

A little later Bowlin was hit in the face with a frag and Fowler was hit in the back of his head and hip by shrapnel. After two and a half hours, they were finally exfilled. This PM we got word that all the WIA are doing okay, including Kris! THANKS TO MAJOR SMITH!!! We put Major Smith in for the Distinguished Service Cross (the Army's second-highest medal, after the Medal of Honor). Most of the recon team was made up of short-timers with thirty days or less! I complained about short-timers being sent out like that, especially when the commanding officer and First Pig knew the area of operations was hot. I'm really pissed. Kris is a very good friend of mine. Kris is also a California boy, and a great guy. I really don't like the commanding officer and First Pig for sending him and the rest of the short-timers out like that.

07 July 1970/Tuesday

Masson and I went down to the creek at the base of the
firebase we are on. The ARVNs use the creek to bathe in
and to fill their water jugs. It was really spooky. We were
over three hundred yards outside the firebase, out of sight
of the firebase, with only my little stinking .32-cal. pistol
and twelve rounds! The ARVNs go all the time without
any trouble, but it gave me the creeps. I've been feeling
sick ever since I got back from the creek. I threw up three
times and have the butt-blasts.

08 July 1970/Wednesday

I was feeling bad all day, so I was flown to the 18th Surgical. I have intestinal flu from bathing with the ARVNs. I'll be spending the night here. I saw Bowlin. All of the WIA from Monday's contact were sent to Japland. Bowlin had shrapnel go through his upper lip, knock out three teeth, and ricochet out the right side of his nose. He's lucky it didn't hit a bone. Kris was blown eight feet into the air and got shrapnel in both calves, thighs, right shoulder, and middle of his chest, puncturing a lung. He's really lucky to be alive. I really thank God Kris is alive! Bowlin said it was really terrible. The recon team was credited with thirteen KIA. Major Smith said there were forty more gunkies moving up the hill to the recon team. They were really lucky! Thank you, God!!!

My second year in the Army!

10 July 1970/Friday

I had a run-in with the First Pig and commanding officer today about going to the bush. I told them they were both stupid for sending half a recon team out to the field with less than thirty days left in country. The First Pig said he was sending me to Company A, 2/501st. The commanding officer said the 501st is looking for a Ranger to teach their Recon Platoon how to run LRRP missions. The 501st just got their butts kicked off Firebase Ripcord, literally. They're both a piece of shit!!! This company has gone down the toilet because of them!

I was coming back into Eagle from the 501st and met Dan Ferrell. We'd gone through Basic Training together. I told him about the crap with the First Pig and the commanding officer, and that I'm being kicked out and sent to the 501st. He said HQ Company, 101st Avn Bn needs a bunker guard NCO. He said that they have been pulling ambushes outside the perimeter of Eagle. That they could use me to teach ambushes. We went right to the First Sergeant and he said he could use me. I went to First Pig Unzicker and he said he had already sent my orders to the 501st.

So I went to the 501st and talked with the executive officer (second in command of a company), Lieutenant Knight. I explained to him the shafting that the First Pig and the commanding officer were doing to me, what they had done to other older Rangers, and what they had done to the company. He didn't seem too impressed with them either. But I explained to him that I had planned to go to the aviation battalion headquarters. I told him I'd been with the Rangers for all this time, working in small teams and having the upper hand. That I only have forty days left in country and can't work as a grunt. He said he hates to lose me, but that he understands. He told me that I would have to have a letter from the aviation battalion headquarters because he had already received the transfer orders from the Rangers. So tomorrow I'll do that.

While I was at the 501st, I talked with the guys there about the Rangers. Four of the guys were interested in transferring. The 501st is returning to the field tomorrow and going back to Firebase Ripcord.

12 July 1970/Sunday

I couldn't find a job yesterday or today because I'm just too short. I had gone to A Troop and was told I didn't have enough time left in country. By the time I got broken in, I'd be going home.

I stopped at the Rangers today to see Burg. Herman Brown had gone on R&R, so I thought I'd spend the night. Burg and I took a shower and then he went to watch a movie.

Stowers came into the hootch I was in with Burg. He asked why I was here, because Dobbs told him I was here. He said I've been kicked out of the company and was not supposed to be back here. I told him I was picking up the last of my trash and visiting Burg. He said that this isn't a hotel, for me to ask next time. I said fine and that I didn't know this was my last day. But that I would ask when I come back. Stowers said okay.

But Chickenshit Dobbs then said that I was told by Top that I couldn't come here. I TOLD Dobbs that all I was told was that I was to sign in and out. I said I didn't know I was officially leaving yet. That I still had tomorrow. Dobbs just said okay and left.

An hour and a half later, Top comes bursting in and tells me to get dressed, that I'm leaving. I got instantly pissed, but Burg grabbed me and said to go ahead and get dressed. Dobbs wasn't satisfied with the commanding officer's dealings with me, so he went and got the First Pig. I was about to pick up my shirt, when the First Pig asked why I haven't changed my LRRP patch to the right sleeve. I was done! I threw my shirt on the floor and told

the First Pig to take my patch off. I was waiting for him
to touch it and I was going to kick him in the face. But
Burg stepped in between us and said for me to stop. The
First Pig wasn't going to pick up the shirt anyway. So I
picked it up and we all walked to the front gate. The First
Pig then said it was all right for me to stay the night as it
was late anyway. I asked him why he didn't say that in the
hootch. He said that I wouldn't have understood. I started
to hit him right there, but Burg grabbed me and spun me
towards the hootch, and off we went. I really didn't think
I had to leave now anyway. The orders weren't in effect
yet. I really hate the COMPANY and First Pig; and
Dobbs too for being such a chickenshit! I feel like kicking all their butts, KIA them, dump them in the bush, get
Ut, and run to the bush and do it my way! The Piss-
ANTS!!!

25 July 1970/Saturday

Went to the Rangers today and the First Pig ASKED me
if I wanted to spend the night! I was shocked! So I did.
Stowers ran into me tonight and asked what I was doing
here. I told him the First Pig invited me. This is really
weird. Burg said it was because he told the First Pig that I
was recruiting for the Rangers. That I'm still a Ranger,
despite being kicked out. I guess some of the guys I had
talked to from the 502d had contacted the First Pig and
asked about joining the Rangers.

26 July 1970/Sunday

At about 1800, it began pouring rain with heavy lightning and thundering (Charlie's weather!). The lightning set off a few claymores in front of Bunker 2. At 1915, lightning exploded some CS in Sector "A" at the bunker line, and the gas came shooting through the Ranger AO. Everybody took off running. We were all in the company club and we all beat feet outside. Some got their gas masks on and the gas blew through. It only lasted about five minutes. But forty-five minutes later, a helluva lot of gas came shooting through. Everybody dashed for the hootches for their masks.

But a lot of us didn't have masks. So we who didn't, just ran for our lives! I was passing people left and right, heading for the aviation company—it was right across the street from the Rangers—to get my mask. I thought I was going to die from taking in so much gas. I was laughing at everybody in a panic over the gas. Guys would fall as they ran and others would just run right by without helping them. I ran past three guys myself. I got to the aviation company and grabbed my mask and went back to the Rangers to help.

When Zen was running, lightning struck right next to him, knocking him to the ground and unconscious and he stopped breathing. MacDaniel (Tex) gave him mouth-to-mouth, and then Zen was taken to the hospital. He's okay now.

It was really pretty funny except for what happened to Zen.

28 July 1970/Tuesday

Today I sacrificed myself by being in an awards cere-
mony. There were nine of us in starched jungles with pistol belts, helmets, and M-16s, standing in a formation
with four other companies of men to watch a three- and a
four-star general give two slick pilots and six crewmen
the Distinguished Flying Cross. I hate ceremonies.

04 August 1970/Tuesday

Burg is going home tomorrow so the Rangers had a farewell party for him. It was a pretty neat party. I'm glad he's going home, but I'm really going to miss him. I really love Burg! He's been a great friend!

05 August 1970/Wednesday

Burg and Brown came by my company and we went to Camp Campbell and saw Burg off. It was really good to see him leave, and in one piece. But I'll really miss him. At least my best friends are home and safe, even though Andy and Kris will struggle for a while. I've lost some really good friends here, but at least Andy and Burg are okay!

When I got back to my company, S.Sgt. May asked me to go on an ambush with him. At 1400, we went on a recon of the area with Russell and four others. It was fun. I wish I had brought my camera. I didn't know it looked like that outside of the perimeter. We went where they had made contact the last time and had gotten three gunkies. We found a good ambush site and returned to Eagle.

06 August 1970/Thursday

34th Mission–N Eagle Perimeter

We left the perimeter at 2000. We had S.Sgt. May, me, Toomey, Spohn, Condon, Bitsilly (Chief), Doc, and Russel. Fifteen minutes out it really got dark and we couldn't find our ambush site. At 2210, we set up in a gravesite, thirty yards off a high-speed trail. Spohn, Toomey, Chief, and I moved about twenty-five yards west and set up. Fifteen minutes later, a gunky set off Condon's claymore, which was on the trail. We then put out our claymores. At about 2400, Spohn spotted a flashlight near his claymore.

07 August 1970/Friday

At 0100, we had five gunkies down below us and three or four near Spohn's claymore. We waited till about 0245, when a gunky cut Spohn's claymore wire. I kept telling Spohn to blow his claymore when he felt someone tugging on it. But he wouldn't. He got up on his knees and tried to see the gunkies. I then told him to throw a frag. I pulled out a grenade and we both then threw frags. But at the same time, the gunkies threw a satchel charge at us that landed a foot and a half from Spohn. He took a frag in his left side, pretty serious. I then opened up with my M-16 in the general direction of where the satchel came from and down to where Spohn's claymore was.

Toomey and Chief grabbed Spohn and I sent my team to May's position. Then May's position began taking satchels and I got one thrown in on me. May took several pieces of shrapnel in his back, but he'll be okay, and I was missed.

While my team ran for May's position, I stayed back and kept firing to cover my team. I then fired my M-79 in several directions, grabbed all the gear the team left behind, and walked to May's position. The reaction force arrived later and Spohn was medevacked, but May refused to go. We then checked the area and found that five of May's claymores had been turned around, facing his team.

There's this Major Clewell here who doesn't believe we were in contact. Damn people piss me off! We faked the WIA too! The shrapnel that Spohn had caught was brought in to us and confirmed to be shrapnel from a gunky frag. That shut the major up. He doesn't like me because I'm a Ranger and he thinks I'm a prima donna.

He heard that I had stayed back by myself to cover my team, and then gathered all the gear left by my team and then just walked to May's position. Spohn will be okay. He goes to Da Nang in three days. I sure wish he had blown his claymore when I told him to!

12 August 1970/Wednesday

I've been at Ut's brother's house with Ut all week. We had gone to the PX and I stole a jeep and drove all the way through to Hue and up the highway to Quang Tri again. What a long drive! I've only taken the trip to Quang Tri by slick and once by Jeep. It only takes about an hour to fly. But driving it took us all stinking day! It was fun, though. We stashed the jeep in a garage. I had a great time. Ut gave me a bracelet as a friendship token. I carried a double-edge diver's knife that I gave to him. I met an old Yard who gave me a homemade crossbow and a bamboo tube with a dozen quarrels in it, all made from bamboo. The string on the bow was a clothesline string. The old man was really neat.

I had a really great time, but I couldn't eat all their food. It is way too spicy. They thought I was pretty funny. I learned that you don't finish all your food though, because they will keep refilling your bowl. I kept telling them that in the USA you are taught to clean your plate, but I couldn't get it through to them. I had a really great time. When I returned to the company I suggested a three-day roving ambush to Top and the commanding officer. I think they liked the idea and will talk it over with Colonel Peachy. I told the commanding officer that I'm here to teach ambushes anyway and it takes more than just giving classes. The commanding officer said he would let me know.

18 August 1970/Tuesday

I was told yesterday to give a briefing today. I gave it to Colonel Peachy, Majors Schneider and Clewell, Sergeant Major Wildt, First Lieutenants Goff and Bacon, and First Sergeant Thurman. I made the operations order as complete as I could, making sure every step was covered. I went into depth with the contacts, tactics, ambushes. It was really fun. At the end they fired all kinds of questions at me, including what I thought about the war, what I've done in the Army and expect to do, why I left the Rangers, and about my home life. It was quite an experience. I felt like I was on a promotion board. The meeting seemed like forever. If everybody listens to Major Clewell, though, I won't be going on the ambush. Colonel Peachy said he would let me know in a couple days.

19 August 1970/Wednesday

Colonel Peachy came to me today and said that my ambush is a go! He asked that I do it really good because there are some here that don't like it. If I do a good job, we'll be able to do more, and it will get Major Clewell off his back. I guess Colonel Peachy can't stand him either. Colonel Peachy said that there were some that really liked my attitude and don't understand why the Rangers kicked me out. I spent all day getting my team together, giving them the operations order, classes, going through drills and equipment together. I'll be drilling them until we leave, which is scheduled for 23 August, Sunday.

22 August 1970/Saturday

We spent a great deal of time learning how to pack our
gear so when we want something, we know where to get
it from everybody's ruck or body. At 1400 was the Miss
America Show. It was pretty neat. The girls were beautiful! I had a run-in with Major Clewell today because I got
either tigers or cammies (camouflage jungle fatigues) for
the team and they are unauthorized for this unit. We got
into a pretty heated argument until we finally went to
Colonel Peachy, who said it was okay for this particular
mission because of the circumstances. Clewell was
pissed. Colonel Peachy told me to try and stay clear of
Clewell, for me to hold my classes somewhere away from
him.

23 August 1970/Sunday

I tested my team and went over last-minute details this
AM, then let them do what they wanted the rest of the afternoon.

35th Mission–Apache

We left the perimeter at 1930, with Russell, me, Walker, Clark, Bednar, and Bitsilly. We went about five hundred meters and set up. Everything was cool during our movement and while setting up. At about 2235, it happened. We first had shadows, then grass moving and twigs breaking around us. I told everybody to just sit still and be patient. At 2305, a gunky was playing with one of Russell's claymores. I called for the reaction force, that we are going to initiate contact, for them to head our way. Unlike Spohn, when I told Russell to blow his claymore, he did, and KIA two. The rest of us threw frags in the direction of the movement. I had everybody throw in a different direction.

We had two frags thrown in at us but no damage. I fired in the direction a frag was thrown from and sprayed a gunky across the chest, KIA him. The reaction force arrived within thirty minutes, and we picked up three bodies and found two blood trails. The reaction force replaced the frags and bullets, then took the bodies and equipment back to Eagle. I had an M-16, and I took the cleanest AK from one of the gunkies and took fifteen mags from the bodies. I gave my M-16 and magazines to the reaction force. I took one magazine bandoleer that a gunky had and put eight magazines in it. I put one more in the AK, and the other six I put into a canteen cover on my war belt. Now I felt good because I had a real gun. We moved about fifty yards in the direction of the blood trails and set up again. Later on, we heard movement from the contact site.

24 August 1970/Monday

We moved at about 0400. We got about twenty-five yards along this ditch where a blood trail had gone and found a body. But there wasn't any equipment on him. We called the reaction force and they policed the body, then they went to the contact site. We hid in some thick trees and bushes for the day and night. It was quiet all night.

25 August 1970/Tuesday

Everything was cool until 0410. Walker was getting his claymore when three gunkies walked up on him. He let them get within eight yards, then opened up. Two gunkies dropped and the other dashed. We didn't know what was going on, and we all dropped. I then ran to Walker. As I was running, a gunky opened up on me and the bullets went a foot to my right and I dived for cover. The gunky started to run and Walker sprayed him across his back, KIA him. When Walker first opened up, he had KIA one gunky and WIA the gunky who shot at me.

The reaction force arrived forty-five minutes later and policed the bodies. I took ten mags off the bodies and put them in canteen pouches on my war belt. We then moved about two hundred fifty meters in the direction the third gunky had run. We set up in some thick bushes and almost got spotted by some villagers about noon. About 1930, we moved west, then north, for four hundred meters, following a high-speed trail with a creek on the side. We set our ambush on the trail. Everything was cool until 2325. Two gunkies carrying AKs walked into our ambush. We blew them away and the reaction force showed up. I told them to only go about five hundred meters and wait because I had a bad feeling. We then moved one hundred meters further and set another ambush.

26 August 1970/Wednesday

At 0200, three gunkies walked into our ambush, but at
the same time, Bednar and Clark, rear security, had
movement by them. I called the reaction force to come
and get us. We then blew the three gunkies away on the
trail. We waited five minutes, when Bednar and Clark
opened up on the gunkies coming up from our rear. They
blew their claymores, KIA two. We then received frags
and AK fire. Clark was WIA with shrapnel in the back of
his right leg, right arm, and back. Russell and I ran to
them, when another frag or RPG came in and landed to
my left front, and blew me backwards into the air. I was
hit in the left knee by a frag that glanced off my knee. It
bled like a stuck pig. I lay there in a daze for what
seemed like a long time, not even hearing the sounds of
the battle. Then Russell bent down over my face and
asked if I was okay. It shook me out of my daze, and I got
up and went to Bednar and Clark. Russell patched up
Clark while Bednar, Bitsilly, Walker, and I put out fire
and frags. The reaction force reached us along with a
Pink Team. After about fifteen minutes of sporadic firing, the gunkies dashed. We searched the area and got six
KIA, three AKs, and an RPG. A medevac took out Clark.
The rest of us walked to the main road (Highway 1) and
were trucked back into Eagle.

I was asked about my knee, but said I'd scraped it
when I fell. When I got back to the company, I was really
bushed. I couldn't believe how tired I was. I told the team
we would have our debrief after noon chow. I then went
and took a shower and slept right through noon chow.

After our debrief, Colonel Peachy congratulated us and then invited us to the Officers Club. It was pretty cool.

I had to give up my AK and magazines I'd gotten. Colonel Peachy said it was a good thing Clewell wasn't here because he would have probably thrown a fit about me using it. We got a total of fifteen gunkies KIA, ten AKs, one RPG, and some papers. The colonels treated us pretty good at the O Club. I think I'm ready to go home now.

27 August 1970/Thursday

I found out Horne's, Tippon's, Thomas', and Haze's recon teams all were in contact during the week. Horne's recon team KIA one gunky; Tippon's recon team was heavy and KIA fifteen (his recon team was credited with seven); Haze's recon team KIA two; and Thomas' recon team had a cherry lieutenant who began arguing with Thomas about which way the recon team should go from the landing zone. While they were arguing, the gunkies hit them and Moss was KIA and the cherry lieutenant WIA! Despite rank, the recon team leader is the boss and runs the recon team, not some snot-nosed officer!

I picked up Ut and we went to A Troop and caught a ride to Quang Tri to Ut's brother's house. It is a whole lot faster by air than by jeep. But it was neat to drive through the towns and country.

01 September 1970/Tuesday

I packed my trash for Camp Campbell today. I should be going to Cam Ranh Bay tomorrow. I stopped by the Rangers today. Haze's recon team is in contact on the landing zone. He was being infilled with two slicks and they were both landing when the gunkies opened up with mortars, .51-cal., and .30-cal. machine guns. One pilot and one door gunner KIA so far. Everybody else is WIA in some way but Haze. All the WIA are serious.

Well, I left for Campbell at 1400 and reached Da Nang, where I have to spend the night. I hate leaving Vietnam on this note! I really feel like staying! But after being burned so bad by the commanding officer and First Pig at the Rangers, I don't see the use. I wish now that I'd have stayed. I would have gone back to the Rangers despite the commanding officer and First Pig! The commanding officer and First Pig have really destroyed the professionalism of the company so bad, it just isn't the same anymore. There are more guys getting KIA and WIA than before. The guys are making contact and having the upper hand, but losing the fights. I don't think my recon team ever lost a fight. I also had one of the highest personal body counts of any Ranger. I just don't like the way the "Mucks" are fighting the war. I did hear that Captain Ohle was going to be the new commanding officer of the Rangers, after Stowers was relieved for his blow-its. I really should have stayed! I loved Captain Ohle and know he will bring back the professionalism we'd lost.

02 September/Wednesday

I left Da Nang early and got to Cam Ranh Bay at 0700. I then filled out papers to go home. After I filled out the papers, I figured this was my chance to extend for six months. But I was told it was too late. I had to do the extension through the Rangers, not here. I was walking around where everybody was sitting and ran into Gregg McGhee! We were both surprised.

He had a rough time. He didn't like the bush, so he re-upped last December to get out of the bush, but ended up back in the bush anyway. He was with the 196th Infantry Brigade, attached to the Americal Division. We then ran into Sergeant Bivens, who had been at Fort Ord with us. He was with the 5th Infantry Division (Mechanized), in Quang Tri.

I did a really stupid thing. I left my carry bag, with my .32-cal. pistol, by my bunk and some turd stole it! I found the bag minus the gun and camera in the latrine. DAMN! When I found it, it was time to load the bird for the World, so I couldn't do anything about it. I was so pissed! I'm used to leaving my stuff lying around at the Rangers and it still being there when I get back to it.

I left Vietnam at 1800. I think I'm going to really miss this place. Colonel Peachy had tried to talk me into extending my tour. He said I could have signed for six months, then got out of the Army completely. That would have been three months short of my regular DEROS. But the Rangers had really burnt me out, and they are the only unit I would go to. I really loved the Rangers and the guys in it. Even those I didn't care too much for, I still liked. We were like family. We could get mad at each other and knock each other, but no one else could, because they aren't Rangers. Only a recon man can knock another recon man. Because only a recon man knows what it's like.

03 September 1970/Thursday

We got to Fort Lewis, Washington, at 0600. We were given a steak dinner and a new set of dress greens. Gregg and I caught a flight to Fresno, where his mom, aunt, and cousin met us. We then drove to his house in Visalia. We bought some funky clothes and went visiting some of his friends. We leave tomorrow for my house. Gregg wants to see his girlfriend who lives in Ontario, next to Pomona.

05 September 1970/Saturday

Left Gregg's house late last night and got to my house at 0430. Gregg went on to Ontario. It was great to be home. When I walked into the house, my family had a big dog. It started barking at me and I yelled at it and it cowered under the kitchen table. The first one I saw was Brad. He's as big as me now. I hardly recognized Jeff. Craig and Laura still look the same. It was great to see my Dad and Mom. I almost started crying. I can hardly believe I'm home. It seems like ages. Vietnam is an experience I will never forget. I got pretty scared towards the end of my tour because of the unprofessionalism of the Rangers, but I definitely learned what I was made of. I know death now and know I won't panic. I'll still be scared, but you're not human if you don't get scared to some degree. But the fear is controllable.

I'm for the war, but there has to be a better way to fight it. Too many soldiers dying because the lifers care more about the equipment than the men. If you're going to fight a war, then fight it, and don't play around with peoples' lives. It seems to be nothing but a game to some.

You can sure tell that money talks in this war! While I was with the Rangers, they had who I considered good leaders in Captain Guy, First Sergeant Gilbert, Lieutenants Johnson and Ohle (later captain), Platoon Sergeants Jefferson, Rocha, and Taylor. Team leaders in Karalow, Black, Davis, Passmore, Bates, Salters, McCoy, Moran, Paige, Yeck, Sands, Horne, etc. I could go on, but we had some really good team leaders. I will never forget the guys, especially Burg, Andy, Bowland, Ut, Kris,

McSorely, Bates, Moran, Mannerburg, Drozd, Dunkle, Strope, Steijen, Jordan, etc.

I could go right down the company roster when I was there. What a unit . . . what a TEAM!!! At the moment it's great to be home and I thank my God for bringing me home safely and in one piece. And for bringing most of my friends home. But I'm really going to miss the camaraderie the most, and the challenges both mental and physical. The memories will stay with me forever, like Dixie, our dog; King Rat, who we used to feed our leftover LRRP meals to when we got back from missions, and who would sit in the middle of the floor and hiss at you if you tried to shoo him away (we found him dead underneath the hootch one day; apparently died from eating poison); the trips to Eagle Beach with the terrorizing rides through Hue on the way back to the company, etc. It was great fun and I'm going to miss the guys the most and the thrill of recon.

I feel like I'm letting the Rangers down by going home. Like our motto says: "RANGERS DON'T LEAVE RANGERS BEHIND!" I feel like I'm leaving them behind by not staying. Especially since I know they could use me right now, that they are struggling and guys are getting hit. I know Captain Ohle needs guys who know what they are doing to get the recon teams functioning like they should. To be an example. I loved the sixth sense that I developed, that I pray I never lose. But again, I miss the camaraderie that I'll probably not find again anywhere.

SURE IS GREAT TO BE HOME THOUGH!!!

THANKS, GOD, IT IS GREAT TO BE HOME!!!

AFTERWORD

As days became weeks and in turn months and then years, American reconnaissance units in Vietnam evolved from an in-country authorized Long-Range Reconnaissance Patrol (LRRP) to Headquarters' DA-sanctioned individual Long-Range Patrol (LRP) units to the individual Ranger companies of the 75th Infantry. As a result of earlier Department of the Army administrative stupidity, which is not uncommon, the history and lineage of Army Rangers was not available to the new units. They were titled under the Combat Arms Regimental System (CARS) with the lineage of Merrill's Marauders, a provisional, conventional infantry unit that fought in an unconventional fashion behind Japanese lines in Burma during World War II. They were not Rangers. No amount of caterwauling will ever make them Rangers, despite their having been awarded the United States Army Ranger tab ex post facto—a military/political act of intrusiveness upon American Ranger History.

As a regiment on paper, with no controlling Headquarters, the individual Ranger companies of the 75th Infantry were left to the mercy of unqualified, disinterested staff officers in the separate brigades and divisions to which the Ranger units were attached for their rations, quarters, and discipline. Like their predecessors, the first Airborne Rangers from the Korean War, the Ranger companies were misused tactically by those who lacked understanding of their capabilities and limitations as light infantry.

Instead of being tasked directly by the S-2/G-2 of the brigades and divisions to operate continuously in the major unit's reconnaissance zone and provide immediate-use combat intelligence and, occasionally, information of strategic importance to the field army, Company L/75th Ranger Infantry was further subordinated to the 2/17th Air Cavalry. This was a tenuous marriage of units with reconnaissance capability but different mission roles. The 101st Airborne Division G-2 wanted no responsibility for the Rangers.

Because of the courage of some individual pilots from the 2/17th Air Cavalry, who sometimes disobeyed the orders of their commander and those of the division commander by claiming radio traffic difficulties, many Ranger teams were rescued, during battles with numerically superior enemy forces, who otherwise would have been left to become carrion at the hands of Vietnamese Communists. These lightly equipped Ranger patrols, composed of six to twelve men, fought alone in battles lasting one to three days, using air and artillery. The pile-on tactics seemed to have been forgotten in the bowels of the Division Tactical Operations bunker. This is interesting as there were days when out of an entire division, hunkered down on firebases and trying to stay alive, only the Rangers were out patrolling and killing the enemy. It must have been embarrassing for the brigade commanders to note during the general's 1700 daily briefing that the only enemy killed that day was by Company L/75th Rangers.

The Ranger patrols were cognizant of the pile-on theory, however. This writer recalls a twelve-man Ranger patrol from Company L/75th being used as the anvil, while a battalion served as the hammer, in a battle against the 5th NVA Regiment. The commanding general was in a snit and fit to be tied because the battalion was still not off the firebase four hours after its appointed LD crossing time. The Rangers had quit using their Personnel Seismic Intrusion Devices (PSID) because they believed they were malfunctioning. A morning check of the adjacent trail revealed that the 5th NVA Regiment had passed by while the battalion was still puttering about on their firebase.

In a designated Airmobile Division, the Ranger company was on short rations when it came to obtaining dedicated aircraft, liftships, or gunships. There should have been birds with volunteer pilots on strip alert for the men who had to infiltrate enemy lines and stay there reconnoitering for five days and four nights. Nothing else was acceptable. This requirement was proven by the predecessor unit in November 1968 when a brigade commander hijacked aircraft dedicated to support the LRPs for his brigade operation. Result? Four dead and eight wounded long-range patrol men. Unnecessary casualties.

No Ranger/pilot bond could possibly be stronger than that of Ranger team leader Marvin Duren (Georgia Peach) and CWO Frederic A. Behrens, a twenty-two-year-old medical evacuation (Dustoff) pilot. Behrens returned to the same hot LZ three times, making two landings before being shot down. His copilot, artillery-man Capt. Roger Madison, revealed that Behrens made a flawless autorotation back into the LZ when his transmission was shot out during takeoff. Madison had no idea that Behrens' foot had been shot off the pedals until six-teen years later. During that three-day battle, Lima Rangers lost one man to POW status (returned) and another to MIA status (James A. Champion, still missing in action).

Cpl. David Quigley, one of five Rangers on the reaction force, said Chief Behrens had so many holes in him that he looked like a piece of Swiss cheese. Wounds did not prevent Behrens from using his Thompson submachine gun. On the morning of 24 April 1971, he dumped half a magazine into a Communist sniper who had just shot Johnnie Sly in the back. The sniper died almost instantly.

The diary of Ranger Frank Johnson is without embellishment. He has sought accuracy by using firsthand encounters, records, and interviews to fill any voids in personal knowledge. Recognized by his peers as fearless, Johnson never displayed foolish bravado. He was considered by many to be "as tough as woodpecker lips."

It was my good fortune to have quality soldiers and Rangers, such as Frank Johnson, assigned to Company L/75th. At a time when they should have been at home dating, dancing, making out, and establishing life's goals, he and others moved silently through the jungles of South

Vietnam in I Corps, kicking ass and taking no names or prisoners, unless so ordered.

Robert F. Gilbert

Robert F. Gilbert
Command Sergeant Major
Infantry, U.S. Army (Ret.)
First Sergeant, L/75th
May 1969–June 1970

GLOSSARY

AA Antiaircraft.

acid pad Helicopter landing pad.

AFB Air Force base.

air burst Explosive device that detonates above ground.

aerial recon Reconning a specific area by helicopter prior to the insertion of a recon patrol.

airstrike Surface attack by fixed-wing fighter/bomber aircraft.

AIT In the U.S. Army, Advanced Individual Training that follows Basic Combat Training.

AK A Soviet-bloc assault rifle, 7.62 cal., also known as the Kalashnikov AK-47.

A Troop or Alpha Troop Letter designation for one of the aerorifle companies of an air cavalry squadron.

AO Area of Operations, specified location established for planned military operations.

ao dai Traditional Vietnamese female dress, split up the sides and worn over pants.

ARA Aerial Rocket Artillery.

ARC Light A B-52 air strike.

Arty fan An area of operations that can be covered by existing artillery support.

ARVN Army of the Republic of (South) Vietnam.

Arty   Artillery.

ATL   Assistant team leader.

A Team   Special Forces operational detachment that normally consists of a single twelve-man team composed of eleven enlisted men and one officer.

bac si   Vietnamese for doctor.

baseball   Baseball-shaped hand grenade with a 5-meter kill range.

BC   Base camp.

BCT   In the U.S. Army, Basic Combat Training every trainee must complete upon entering service.

BDA   Bomb Damage Assessment.

beat feet   Running from danger.

beaucoup or boo koo   French for "many."

beehive   Artillery round filled with hundreds of small metal darts designed to be used against massed infantry.

berm   Built-up earthen wall used for defensive purposes.

Bird Dog   A small fixed-wing observation plane.

black box   Sensor device that detects body heat or movement. They were buried along routes used by the enemy to record their activity in the area.

black PJs   A type of local garb of Vietnamese farmers, also worn extensively by Viet Cong guerrillas.

blasting cap   A small device inserted into an explosive substance that can be triggered to cause the detonation of the main charge.

blood trail   Spoor sign left by the passage or removal of enemy wounded or dead.

Blues   Another name for the aerorifle platoons or troops of an air cavalry squadron.

body bag   A thick black plastic bag used to transport American and allied dead to Graves Registration points.

B Troop or Bravo Troop   Letter designation for one of the air-rifle companies of an air cavalry squadron.

break contact   Disengaging from battle with an enemy unit.

bring smoke   Placing intensive fire upon the enemy. Killing the enemy with a vengeance.

bush   The jungle.

buy the farm   To die.

C-4   A very stable, pliable plastique explosive.

C's   Combat field rations for American troops.

C&C   Command and Control.

CA   Combat assault.

cammies   Jungle-patterned clothing worn by U.S. troops in the field.

cammo stick   Two-colored camouflage applicator.

CAR-15   Carbine version of the M-16 rifle.

Cav   Cavalry.

CCN   Command and Control (North), MACV-SOG.

Charlie, Charles, Chuck   G.I. slang for VC/NVA.

cherry   New arrival in country.

Chi-Com   Chinese Communist.

chieu hoi   Government program that encouraged enemy soldiers to come over to the South Vietnam side.

Chinook   CH-47 helicopter used for transporting equipment and troops.

chopper   G.I. slang for helicopter.

chopper pad   Helicopter landing pad.

CIDG   Civilian Irregular Defense Group. South Vietnamese or Montagnard civilians trained and armed to defend themselves against enemy attack.

clacker   Firing device used to manually detonate a claymore mine.

CO   Commanding officer.

Cobra   AH-IG attack helicopter.

cockadau   G.I. slang for the Vietnamese word meaning "kill."

Col. Abbreviation for the rank of Colonel.

cold An area of operations or a recon zone is "cold" if it is unoccupied by the enemy.

commo Communication by radio or field telephone.

commo check A radio/telephone operator requesting confirmation of his own transmission.

compromise Discovered by the enemy.

contact Engaged by the enemy.

CP Command post.

Cpt. Abbreviation for the rank of Captain.

CS Riot gas.

daisy chain Wiring a number of claymore mines together with det cord to achieve a simultaneous detonation.

debrief The gleaning of information and intelligence after a military operation.

DEROS The date of return from an overseas tour of duty.

det cord Timed burn-fuse used to detonate an explosive charge.

didi Vietnamese for to run or move quickly.

diddy boppin' Moving foolishly, without caution.

DMZ Demilitarized Zone.

Doc A medic or doctor.

dong lai Vietnamese for "don't move."

double canopy Jungle or forest with two layers of overhead vegetation.

Doughnut Dollies Red Cross hostesses.

drag The last man on a long range reconnaissance patrol.

Dustoff Medical evacuation by helicopter.

DZ Drop zone for airborne parachute operation.

E&E Escape and Evasion, on the run to evade pursuit and capture.

E-1 or E-2 Military pay grades of Private.

E-3 Military pay grade of Private First Class.

E-4   Military pay grade of Specialist Fourth Class or Corporal.

E-5   Military pay grade of Specialist Fifth Class or Sergeant.

E-6   Military pay grade of Specialist Sixth Class or Staff Sergeant.

E-7   Military pay grade of Sergeant First Class or Platoon Sergeant.

E-8   Military pay grade of Master Sergeant or First Sergeant.

E-9   Military pay grade of Sergeant Major.

ER   Enlisted Reserve.

ETS   Estimated Termination of Service.

exfil   Extraction from a mission or operation.

extension leave   A 30-day furlough given at the end of a full tour of duty after which the recipient must return for an extended tour of duty.

FAC   Forward Air Controller. Air Force spotter plane that coordinated airstrikes and artillery for ground units.

fast mover   Jet fighter/bomber.

fire base   Forward artillery position usually located on a prominent terrain feature used to support ground units during operations.

finger   A secondary ridge running out from a primary ridgeline, a hill, or a mountain.

firefight   A battle with an enemy force.

fire mission   A request for artillery support.

fix   The specific coordinates pertaining to a unit's position or to a target.

flare ship   Aircraft used to drop illumination flares in support of ground troops in contact at night.

flash panel   A fluorescent orange or yellow cloth used to mark a unit's position for supporting or inbound aircraft.

field   Anywhere outside "friendly" control.

FO   Forward Observer. A specially trained soldier, usually an officer, attached to an infantry unit for the purpose of coordinating close artillery support.

FNG   "Fucking New Guy." Slang term for a recent arrival in Vietnam.

foo gas or phou gas   A jellied gasoline explosive that is buried in a 55-gallon drum along defensive perimeters. When detonated, it sends out a wall of highly flammable fuel similar to napalm.

freak or freq   Slang term meaning a radio frequency.

ghost or ghost time   Taking time off, free time, goofing off.

grazing fire   Keeping the trajectory of bullets between normal knee to waist height.

grease   Slang term meaning "to kill."

Green Beret   A member of the U.S. Army Special Forces.

groundpounder   Infantryman.

grunt   Infantryman.

G-2   Division or larger operations section.

G-3   Division or larger intelligence section.

gook   Derogatory slang for VC/NVA.

gunk, gunkies   Derogatory slang for VC/NVA.

gunship   An armed attack helicopter.

HE   High explosive.

H&I   Harassment and Interdiction. Artillery fire upon certain areas of suspected enemy travel or rally points, designed to prevent uncontested use.

heavy team   In a long range patrol unit, two five- or six-man teams operating together.

helipad   A hardened helicopter landing pad.

Ho Chi Minh Trail   An extensive road and trail network running from North Vietnam, down through Laos and Cambodia into South Vietnam, which enabled the North Vietnamese to supply equipment and personnel to their units in South Vietnam.

hootch   Slang for barracks or living quarters.

horn   Radio or telephone handset.

hot   A landing zone or drop zone under enemy fire.

HQ   Headquarters.

Huey   The Bell UH helicopter series.

hug   To close with the enemy in order to prevent his use of supporting fire.

hump   Patrolling or moving during a combat operation.

I Corp   The northernmost of the four separate military zones in South Vietnam. The other divisions were II, III, and IV Corps.

infil   Insertion of a recon team or military unit into a recon zone or area of operation.

Indian Country   Territory under enemy control.

Immersion foot   A skin condition of the feet caused by prolonged exposure to moisture that results in cracking, bleeding, and sloughing of skin.

incoming   Receiving enemy indirect fire.

indigenous   Native peoples.

intel   Information on the enemy gathered by human, electronic, or other means.

Jungle penetrator   A metal cylinder, lowered by cable from a helicopter, used to extract personnel from inaccessible terrain.

KIA   Killed in Action.

Killer team   A small Lurp/Ranger team with the mission of seeking out and destroying the enemy.

LAW   Light Anti-tank Weapon.

lay dog   Slang meaning "to go to cover and remain motionless while listening for the enemy." This is SOP for a recon team immediately after being inserted or infilled.

LBJ   Long Bien Jail. The in-country military stockade for U.S. Army personnel convicted of violations of the U.S. Code of Military Justice.

LDR   Leader.

Lifer   Slang for career soldier.

LMG   Light machine gun.

LOH or Loach   OH-6A light observation helicopter.

LP   Listening post. An outpost established beyond the perimeter wire, manned by one or more personnel with the mission of detecting approaching enemy forces before they can launch an assault.

LRP   Long Range Patrol.

LRRP   Long Range Reconnaissance Patrol.

Lt.   Lieutenant.

Lt. Col.   Lieutenant Colonel.

LZ   Landing zone. A cleared area large enough to accommodate the landing of one or more helicopters.

MAAG   Military Assistance Advisory Group. The senior U.S. military headquarters during the early American involvement in Vietnam.

MACV   Military Assistance Command Vietnam. The senior U.S. military headquarters after full American involvement in the war.

MACV Recondo school   A three-week school conducted at Nha-trang, South Vietnam, by cadre from the 5th Special Forces Group to train U.S. and allied reconnaissance personnel in the art of conducting long-range patrols.

MACV-SOG   Studies and Observations Group under command of MACV that ran long-range reconnaissance and other classified missions over the borders of South Vietnam into NVA sanctuaries in Laos and Cambodia.

mag   Short for magazine.

Maguire Rig   A single rope with loops at the end that

could be dropped from a helicopter to extract friendly personnel from inaccessible terrain.

Main Force Full-time Viet Cong military units, as opposed to local, part-time guerrilla units.

Maj. Major.

Marine Force Recon U.S. Marine Corps divisional long range reconnaissance units similar in formation and function to U.S. Army LRP/Ranger companies.

Medevac or Dustoff Medical evacuation by helicopter.

MG Machine gun.

MIA Missing in Action.

Mike Force Special Forces mobile strike force used to reinforce or support other Special Forces units or camps under attack.

Montagnard The tribal hill people of Vietnam.

MOS Military Occupation Skill.

MP Military Police.

MPC Military Payment Certificates. Paper money issued U.S. military personnel serving overseas in lieu of local or U.S. currency.

M-14 The standard issue 7.62 mm semiautomatic/automatic rifle used by U.S. military personnel prior to the M-16.

M-16 The standard issue 5.56 mm semiautomatic/automatic rifle that became the mainstay of U.S. ground forces in 1967.

M-60 A light 7.62 mm machine gun that has been the primary infantry automatic weapon of U.S. forces since the Korean War.

M-79 An individually operated, single-shot 40mm grenade launcher.

NCO Noncommissioned officer.

NDP Night defensive position.

net   Radio network.

NG   National Guard.

no sweat   With little effort or with no trouble.

Number One   The best or highest possible.

Number Ten   The worst or lowest possible.

nuoc mam   Strong, evil-smelling fish sauce used to add flavor to the standard Vietnamese food staple—rice.

Nungs   Vietnamese troops of Chinese extraction hired by U.S. Special Forces to serve as personal bodyguards and to man special strike units and recon teams. Arguably the finest indigenous forces in Vietnam.

NVA   North Vietnamese Army.

OP   Observation post. An outpost established on a prominent terrain feature for the purpose of visually observing enemy activity.

op   Operation.

op order   Operations order. A plan for a mission or operation to be conducted against enemy forces, covering all facets of such mission or operation.

overflight   An aerial reconnaissance of an intended recon zone or area of operation prior to the mission or operation, for the purpose of selecting access and egress points, routes of travel, likely enemy concentrations, water, and prominent terrain features.

P-38   Standard manual can opener that comes with government-issued C rations.

P's or piasters   South Vietnamese monetary system. During the height of the Vietnam war, 100P was equal to about $0.85 U.S.

P training   Preparatory training. A one-week course required for each new U.S. Army soldier arriving in South Vietnam, designed to acclimatize new arrivals to weather conditions and give them a basic introduction to the enemy and his tactics.

pen flare A small spring-loaded, cartridge-fed signal flare device that fired a variety of small colored flares used to signal one's position.

peter pilot Military slang for the assistant- or copilot on a helicopter.

Pfc. Private First Class.

Pink Team An aviation combat patrol package composed of an LOH scout helicopter and a Charlie model Huey gunship or an AH-1G Cobra. The LOH would fly low to draw enemy fire and mark its location for an immediate strike from the gunship circling high overhead.

pith helmet A light tropical helmet worn by some NVA units.

pork chop A bad deal, destined for failure.

POW Prisoner of War.

PRC-10 or "Prick Ten" Standard issue platoon/company radio used early in the Vietnam War.

PRC-25 or "Prick Twenty-five" Standard issue platoon/company radio that replaced the PRC-10.

PRC-74 Heavier, longer range radio capable of voice or code communication.

Project Delta Special Forces special unit tasked to conduct long-range patrols in Southeast Asia.

Project Gamma Special Forces special unit tasked to conduct long-range patrols in Southeast Asia.

Project Sigma Special Forces special unit tasked to conduct long-range patrols in Southeast Asia.

PRU Provincial Reconnaissance Units. Mercenary soldiers who performed special military tasks throughout South Vietnam. Known for their effective participation in the Phoenix Program, where they used prisoner snatches and assassinations to destroy the VC infrastructure.

PSP   Perforated Steel Panels used to build airstrips, landing pads, bridge surfaces, and a number of other functions.

point   The point man or lead soldier in a patrol.

Puff the Magic Dragon   AC-47 or AC-119 aircraft armed with computer-controlled miniguns that rendered massive support to fixed friendly camps and infantry units under enemy attack.

pulled   Extracted or exfilled.

punji stakes   Sharpened bamboo stakes, imbedded in the ground at an angle designed to penetrate into the foot or leg of anyone walking into one. Often poisoned with human excrement to cause infection.

Purple Heart   A U.S. medal awarded for receiving a wound in combat.

PX   Post Exchange.

radio relay   A communications team located in a position to relay radio traffic between two points.

R&R   Rest and Recreation. A short furlough given U.S. forces while serving in a combat zone.

Rangers   Designation for U.S. long range reconnaissance patrollers after 31 January 1969.

rappel   Descent from a stationary platform or a hovering helicopter by sliding down a harness-secured rope.

reaction force   Special units designed to relieve a small unit in heavy contact.

redleg   Military slang for artillery.

REMF   Rear Echelon Mother Fucker. Military slang for rear echelon personnel.

rock and roll   Slang for firing one's weapon on full automatic.

Round-Eye   Slang for a non-Asian female.

RPD/RPK   Soviet-bloc light machine gun.

RPG   Soviet-bloc front-loaded anti-tank rocket launcher used effectively against U.S. bunkers, armor, and infantry during the Vietnam War.

rear security   The last man on a long range reconnaissance patrol.

RT   Recon Team.

RTO   Radio/telephone operator.

ruck   Rucksack or backpack.

Ruff-Puff or RF   South Vietnamese regional and popular forces recruited to provide security in hamlets, villages, and within districts throughout South Vietnam. A militia-type force that was usually ineffective.

saddle up   Preparing to move out on patrol.

same-same   The same as.

sapper   VC/NVA soldiers trained to penetrate enemy defense perimeters and to destroy fighting positions, fuel and ammo dumps, and command and communication centers with demolition charges, usually prior to a ground assault by infantry.

satchel charge   Explosive charge usually carried in a canvas bag across the chest and activated by a pull cord. The weapon of the sapper.

Screaming Chickens or Puking Buzzards   Slang for members of the 101st Airborne Division.

SEALs   Small U.S. Navy special operations units trained in reconnaissance, ambush, prisoner snatch, and counterguerrilla techniques.

search & destroy   Offensive military operation designed to seek out and eradicate the enemy.

SERTS   Screaming Eagle Replacement Training School. Rear area indoctrination course that introduced newly arrived 101st Airborne Division replacements to the rigors of combat in Vietnam.

SF   U.S. Special Forces or Green Berets.

SFC. Sergeant First Class (E-7).

Sgt. Sergeant.

shake 'n' bake A graduate of a stateside noncommissioned or commissioned officer's course.

short timer Anyone with fewer than 30 days left in his combat tour.

short rounds Artillery rounds that impact short of their target.

single canopy Jungle or forest with a single layer of trees.

sit rep Situation Report. A radio or telephone transmission, usually to a unit's tactical operations center to provide information on that unit's current status.

Six Designated call sign for a commander, such as "Alpha-Six."

SKS Communist bloc semiautomatic rifle.

sky To run or flee because of enemy contact.

slack Slang for the second man in a patrol formation. The point man's backup.

slick Slang for a lightly armed Huey helicopter primarily used to transport troops.

smoke A canister-shaped grenade that dispenses smoke, used to conceal a unit from the enemy or to mark a unit's location for aircraft. The smoke comes in a variety of colors.

Snake Cobra helicopter gunship.

snatch To capture a prisoner.

Sneaky Pete A member of an elite military unit who operates behind enemy lines.

snoop and poop A slang term meaning "to gather intelligence in enemy territory and get out again without being detected."

socked in Unable to be resupplied or extracted due to inclement weather.

SOI Signal Operations Instructions. The classified code book that contains radio frequencies and call signs.

Sp4. or Spec Four Specialist fourth class (E-4).

Spectre An AC-130 aircraft gunship armed with mini-guns, Vulcans, and sometimes a 105mm howitzer with the mission of providing close ground support for friendly ground troops.

spider hole A camouflaged one-man fighting position frequently used by the VC/NVA.

Spooky AC-47 or AC-119 aircraft armed with Gatling guns and capable of flying support over friendly positions for extended periods. Besides serving as an aerial weapons platform, Spooky was capable of dropping illumination flares.

spotter round An artillery smoke or white phosphorus round that was fired to mark a position.

S.Sgt. Staff Sergeant (E-6).

staging area An area in the rear where final last-minute preparations for an impending operation or mission are conducted.

stand-down A period of rest after completion of a mission or operation in the field.

star cluster An aerial signal device that produces three individual flares. Comes in red, green, or white.

starlight scope A night-vision device that utilizes any outside light source for illumination.

Stars and Stripes U.S. military newspaper.

stay behind A technique involving a small unit dropping out of or remaining behind when its larger parent unit moves out on an operation. A method of inserting a recon team.

strobe light A small device employing a highly visible, bright flashing light used to identify one's position at night. Normally used only in emergency situations.

TA Target Area. Another designation for AO or area of operations.

TAOR   Tactical Area of Responsibility. Another designation for a unit's area of operations.

TAC Air   Tactical air support.

tail gunner   Rear security or the last man in a patrol.

TDY   Temporary duty.

tee tee or ti ti   Very small.

ten forty-nine or 1049   Military Form 1049 used to request a transfer to another unit.

thumper or thump gun   Slang terms for the M-79 grenade launcher.

Tiger Force   The battalion reconnaissance platoon of the 1/327, 101st Airborne Division.

tigers or tiger fatigues   Camouflage pattern of black and green stripes usually worn by reconnaissance teams or elite units.

time pencil   A delayed-fuse detonating device attached to an explosive charge or a claymore antipersonnel mine.

TL   Team leader.

TM   Team.

TOC   Tactical Operations Center or command center of a military unit.

toe popper   Small-pressure detonated antipersonnel mine intended to maim, not kill.

Top   Slang term for a First Sergeant meaning "top" NCO.

tracker   Soldiers specializing in trailing or tracking the enemy.

triple canopy   Jungle or forest that has three distinct layers of trees.

troop   Slang term for a soldier, or a unit in a cavalry squadron equal to an infantry company in size.

Tri-Border   The area in Indochina where Laos, Cambodia, and South Vietnam come together.

tunnel rat   A small-statured U.S. soldier who is sent into underground enemy tunnel complexes armed only with a flashlight, a knife, and a pistol.

URC10   A pocket-sized, short-range emergency radio.

VC   Viet Cong. South Vietnamese communist guerrillas.
Viet Minh   Short for Vietnam Doc Lap Dong Minh, or
League for the Independence of Vietnam. Organized by
communist sympathizers who fought against the Japanese
and later the French.
VNSF   South Vietnamese Special Forces.

warning order   The notification, prior to an op order,
given to a recon team to begin preparation for a mission.
waste   To kill the enemy by any means available.
White Mice   Derogatory slang term for South Vietnamese
Army MPs.
WIA   Wounded in Action.
World   Slang term for the United States of America or
"home."
WP or willie pete   White phosphorus grenade.

XF   Exfil. Extraction from the field, usually by helicopter.
xin loi/sin loi   Vietnamese for "sorry" or "too bad."
XO   Executive officer.
x-ray team   A communication team established at a site
between a remote recon patrol and its TOC. Its function is
to assist in relaying messages between the two stations.

Yards   Short for Montagnards.

zap   To kill or wound.